Persian Mythology

Captivating Myths of Gods, Goddesses, Heroes, and Legendary Creatures

© Copyright 2021

The contents of this book may not be reproduced, duplicated, or transmitted without direct written permission from the author.

Under no circumstances will any legal responsibility or blame be held against the publisher for any reparation, damages, or monetary loss due to the information herein, either directly or indirectly.

Legal Notice:

This book is copyright protected. This is only for personal use. You cannot amend, distribute, sell, use, quote, or paraphrase any part of the content within this book without the consent of the author.

Disclaimer Notice:

Please note the information within this document is for educational and entertainment purposes only. Every attempt has been made to provide accurate, up to date, and reliable complete information. No warranties of any kind are expressed or implied. Readers acknowledge that the author is not engaging in the rendering of legal, financial, medical, or professional advice. The content of this book has been derived from various sources. Please consult a licensed professional before attempting any techniques outlined in this book.

By reading this document, the reader agrees that under no circumstances is the author responsible for any losses, direct or indirect, which are incurred because of the use of the information within this document, including, but not limited to, errors, omissions, or inaccuracies.

Free Bonus from Captivating History (Available for a Limited time)

Hi History Lovers!

Now you have a chance to join our exclusive history list so you can get your first history ebook for free as well as discounts and a potential to get more history books for free! Simply visit the link below to join.

Captivatinghistory.com/ebook

Also, make sure to follow us on Facebook, Twitter and Youtube by searching for Captivating History.

Contents

INTRODUCTION 1
PART I: RELIGIOUS MYTHS 4
PART II: BAKHTIYAR NAMEH 19
PART III: TALES FROM THE SHAHNAMEH 45
HERE'S ANOTHER BOOK BY MATT CLAYTON THAT YOU MIGHT LIKE 87
FREE BONUS FROM CAPTIVATING HISTORY (AVAILABLE FOR A LIMITED TIME) 88
BIBLIOGRAPHY 89

Introduction

The Persian Empire was one of the most powerful in the ancient world. Under the Achaemenids, between 500 and 330 BCE, it encompassed a large part of Southwestern Central Asia, including what are now Iran and Afghanistan, and parts of Southern Greece, Eastern Libya and Egypt, the Levant, and part of the Northern Saudi Arabian peninsula. However, at its core was the land that is now Iran, home to some of the world's oldest cultures.

By the third millennium BCE, what was to become Persia became occupied by people who migrated into that area from India. These people called themselves "Aryans," an ancient word in the Avestan language that denotes this particular cultural group and is the root of modern Iran's name.

(Note: The name of this ancient culture has nothing to do with the Third Reich or white supremacist ideology; the word was appropriated for racist uses by Europeans in the nineteenth century.)

The ancient Aryan people kept many of the religious practices and concepts with which they had been familiar in their former home, and these became integrated into the native Persian religion of Zoroastrianism, which was founded c. 1500-1000 BCE by Zarathustra (aka Zoroaster), a man who purported to have had a vision of Ahura Mazda, the Aryan chief god. Zoroastrianism is essentially dualist, positing Ahura Mazda (Middle Persian "Ohrmazd") as a beneficent creator who vies with Angra Mainyu (Middle Persian "Ahriman"), an evil being whose purpose is to mar and destroy anything made by Ahura Mazda. Zoroastrianism became the official Persian state religion c. 600 BC and is still practiced today, mostly in Iran and India, where it is a minority religion.

Zoroastrian sacred writings are the chief repository of ancient Persian religious myths. Initially, Zoroastrian teachings were transmitted orally; the earliest written texts seem to have been collated during the Sassanian Empire (224-621CE), but the oldest surviving copy is much later, dating from the fourteenth century. The primary collection of these writings is known as the *Avesta* (sometimes called the *Zend-Avesta*), which contains instructions for the performance of religious ceremonies, prayers, moral instruction, sacred laws, and myths concerning Ahura Mazda, Angra Mainyu, and the other sacred cosmic beings who play roles within Zoroastrian religious traditions. The first section of this book is dedicated to Zoroastrian religious tales, both from the *Avesta* and the later *Bundahisn*, another important Zoroastrian sacred document.

Another primary source of ancient Persian myth is the *Shahnameh*, which means "tales of the kings." The *Shahnameh* was compiled between 997 and 1010 CE by Persian poet Abdul Qasem Ferdowsi Tusi (c. 935 or 940-c. 1019 or 1026; often called simply "Ferdowsi"). In its original form, *Shahnameh* is an epic poem that relates the history of the Persian kings, beginning with the earliest mythical rulers and ending with historically accurate tales about the Sasanian Empire. These stories are full of kings' and heroes' exploits, the misdeeds of demons, battles, dragons, and derring-do, making for lively reading. The first few tales in the *Shahnameh* also function as just-so stories, explaining the origins of many human activities and practices, attributed to the wisdom and intelligence of early mythical kings. The tour through Persian myth ends with selections from

Ferdowsi's collection of stories, including "The Seven Trials of Rostam," a lengthy tale about the deeds of the most famous and important of all ancient Persian heroes, and his faithful steed, Rakhsh.

In between the sacred stories from the *Avesta* and *Bundahisn* and the secular tales of the *Shahnameh* is an extended excerpt from the *Bakhtiyar Nameh*. The *Bakhtiyar Nameh*, which was compiled in the late sixth or early seventh century CE, consists of a frame story that narrates the life of Bakhtiyar, the title character, in between the sections of which are sandwiched nine folktales told by Bakhtiyar to King Azadbakht. Readers who are familiar with the story of Scheherezade and the tales of the *Arabian Nights* will recognize this structure—since both Scheherezade and Bakhtiyar are characters set within a frame narrative who attempt to save their lives by telling stories to a monarch who means to kill them. However, this is not the sole link between these two pieces of literature; characters from the *Bakhtiyar Nameh*, particularly King Azadbakht, also appear in the later *Arabian Nights* collection.

Persian myth's cultural roots are deep, going back more than five thousand years, stemming as they do from the original Aryan culture in its Indian homeland, which was later transplanted to and transformed on the Iranian Plateau. The Persian religious thought that grew out of ancient Aryan culture is rich in its own right and had important and lasting influences on Judaism, Christianity, and Islam. Persian sacred myth provides yet another fascinating look at how human beings have understood the structure of the universe and their place within it, while secular tales of heroes and kings allow one to escape into a land that is simultaneously mythical and historical, in which demons and dragons always get their comeuppance, and good always wins the day.

Part I: Religious Myths

The Myth of Yima

The myth of Yima is preserved in the Vendidad section of the Zoroastrian holy text, Zend-Avesta. As with many other sections of the Avesta, this story is framed as a dialogue between the good god Ahura Mazda and the prophet Zarathustra. Yima's story functions both as a creation myth and a flood myth since once Yima has finished his work of enlarging the created world, Ahura Mazda tells him to save the people, plants, and animals from the coming apocalyptic winter. In addition, the story also sets up Zarathustra as a kind of successor to Yima since Yima initially refuses Ahura Mazda's call to be a lawgiver and a prophet, duties that are conferred upon Zarathustra at the very end of the myth. (In the retelling below, the myth is presented without the Zoroastrian framing.)

In his work of enlarging the created world, Yima calls upon the power of the Spenta Armaiti. The six Spentas were manifestations of the power of Ahura Mazda, and each one had different qualities. The Spenta Armaiti was a feminine aspect of the divine and associated with religious devotion, devotion to the family, and the earth. The myth also references Vivahvant, an ancient Indo-Iranian sun deity (Vivasvat in India) who is said to be the father of Yima.

This myth mentions a place called Airyanem Vaejah, considered to be the ancient, original home of the Iranian people. Although in the Avesta, Airyanem Vaejah takes on mythical qualities, it appears to have been a real place. Many theories have been advanced as to where Airyanem Vaejah actually was, and while scholars disagree on an exact location, many agree that Airyanem Vaejah probably was somewhere in central Asia, perhaps in what is now Afghanistan or Kazakhstan.

When Ahura Mazda, the good god, had created the world and begun to people it, he went to Yima, the good shepherd, and said, "O Yima, son of Vivahvant, I, Ahura Mazda, ask you: Will you go among the people and teach them my religion?"

"O Ahura Mazda, I was not made for this task. I cannot teach the people your religion," said Yima.

"Very well," said Ahura Mazda. "If you will not be the teacher of my religion, then you will increase the world I have made, and you will enlarge it. You will be the protector and guardian of my world."

"That I will do gladly. I will be the protector and guardian of your world, and I will enlarge it and increase it. While I reign, there will be neither disease nor death, neither cold wind nor hot wind."

"It is well." Ahura Mazda gave Yima a golden seal and golden spear.

Yima ruled the world for three hundred years, and at the end of that time, Ahura Mazda looked down upon the earth and saw that it was full of herds and flocks, birds and dogs, and people and blazing red fires.

Ahura Mazda then went to Yima and said, "O Yima, son of Vivahvant, there is no more room in the world I have made."

So, Yima went forth to the south, following the path of the Sun.

He smote the earth with his golden seal and pierced it with his golden spear, saying, "O Spenta Armaiti, O Spirit of Holy Devotion, hear me! Open yourself! Stretch yourself! Make more room for herds and flocks, birds and dogs, people, and blazing red fires!"

Spenta Armaiti heard Yima's prayer, and the earth became larger than it had been by one third, and now there was more room for all the creatures.

Yima ruled over the world for six hundred years, and in that time, the world once again became full of herds and flocks, birds and dogs, and people and blazing red fires.

Ahura Mazda looked down and saw that the world he had created was full with no more room upon it, so Ahura Mazda then went to Yima and said, "O Yima, son of Vivahvant, there is no more room in the world I have made."

So, Yima went forth to the south, following the path of the Sun.

He smote the earth with his golden seal and pierced it with his golden spear, saying, "O Spenta Armaiti, O Spirit of Holy Devotion, hear me! Open yourself! Stretch yourself! Make more room for herds and flocks, birds and dogs, people, and blazing red fires!"

Spenta Armaiti heard Yima's prayer, and the earth became larger than it had been by two thirds, and now there was more room for all the creatures.

Yima ruled over the world for nine hundred years, and in that time, the world once again became full of herds and flocks, birds and dogs, and people and blazing red fires.

Ahura Mazda looked down and saw that the world he had created was full with no more room upon it, so Ahura Mazda then went to Yima and said, "O Yima, son of Vivahvant, there is no more room in the world I have made."

So, Yima went forth to the south, following the path of the Sun. He smote the earth with his golden seal and pierced it with his golden spear, saying, "O Spenta Armaiti, O Spirit of Holy Devotion, hear me! Open yourself! Stretch yourself! Make more room for herds and flocks, birds and dogs, people, and blazing red fires!"

Spenta Armaiti heard Yima's prayer, and the earth became larger than it had been by three thirds, and now there was more room for all the creatures.

There came a time when Ahura Mazda called together a council of all the good yazatas—the angels who do Ahura Mazda's will—and to this council also came Yima and all the best men of Airyanem Vaejah, through which flows the good Daiti River.

When all were assembled, Ahura Mazda said, "Hearken unto me, O Yima, the good shepherd of the earth! Winter is coming to the earth, and it will cover it with snow. This winter will kill two-thirds of the cattle, and when the snow melts, it will create rushing waters that will wash everything away.

"O Yima, son of Vivahvant, you must make a safe place for the people and the flocks, for the animals and the birds. Give that place four sides, and make each side the length of a stadium. Within this place bring the best of the people and the flocks. Let none be marred by disease or misfortune. Bring seeds of plants and crops and trees, bring dogs and birds. Bring red burning fires. Make a stream run through this place, and build dwellings and streets. In this place, let there be no strife and no enmity, no poverty and no disease, no spite and no falsehood. In this place, food will always be plentiful. Use the golden lance to shepherd all into this place, and then build a wall around it, with windows to give light."

Then Yima said, "O mighty Ahura Mazda, how am I to make this place according to your command?"

Ahura Mazda replied, "Trample the earth with your feet, and strike it with your hands, and the earth shall open up and provide the place to you."

Yima did as Ahura Mazda commanded. He made the safe place to be the length of a stadium on all four sides, and into that place, he brought the best of the people and the flocks, the seeds of plants and crops and trees, dogs and birds, and red burning fires. He built dwellings and streets, and in that place, there was neither strife nor enmity, neither poverty nor disease, neither spite nor falsehood, and food was always plentiful. Then, he built a wall around it and put windows into the wall to give light.

In this safe place that Yima made, there are also the Sun, Moon, and stars, and to those who dwell within this place, a year seems like a day. Every forty years, the people and the animals will give birth to twins, a boy and a girl, and all within this place live the very best of lives.

Angra Mainyu and Zarathustra

The nineteenth fargard (section or chapter) of the Avesta is dedicated to the tale of how Angra Mainyu and his demons attempted to kill Zarathustra but were forced to flee because of his holiness. This fargard also contains lists of invocations that are supposed to drive away evil forces and give detailed instructions for rituals of sacrifice and purification. (For this book, the lists of invocations have been truncated and the instructions concerning rituals omitted.)

This fargard also mentions the Saoshyant, whose name means "one who brings benefit." According to Zoroastrian belief, the Saoshyant will appear at the end of the world and rid creation of all evil, and he will come from Zarah Lake. However, another Zoroastrian belief states that there will be three Saoshyants, one for each three-thousand-year period of history, during which the struggle between Ahura Mazda and the forces of evil play out. The exact location of Zarah Lake is unknown, but some scholars place it in modern-day Afghanistan.

Out of the far north came Angra Mainyu, the Evil One, the king of the demons, and he said, "O Druj! Go you and smite the holy Zarathustra! Kill him!"

And so, the Druj, which is the demon Buiti, the demon of death, and a company of demons went to do Angra Mainyu's bidding.

When Zarathustra saw that the demons were there to kill him, he recited the Ahuna Vairya, the great prayer to Ahura Mazda.

The demons heard Zarathustra's prayer and fled in dismay.

The demons went to Angra Mainyu and said, "O tormenter! We cannot kill the holy Zarathustra. Death has no hold on him."

Zarathustra knew that the demons were plotting to kill him; he saw this within his soul. So, Zarathustra set out in search of Angra Mainyu, and on the way, he picked up many large stones, which were provided to him by the holy Ahura Mazda.

Angra Mainyu saw Zarathustra approaching with the great stones in his hands and said, "O Zarathustra, where are you going with those large stones in your hands?"

Zarathustra replied, "O Evil One! O Angra Mainyu! I am going to smite all your evil creations. I will smite the demons and the Nasu, the demon of rotting corpses. I will strike down idolatry. This I will do until the coming of the holy Saoshyant, who shall be born out of the waters of the Zarah Lake, who shall come out of the regions of the east."

"Do not smite my demons, O Zarathustra! Your father was Pourushaspa, and your mother worshiped me. Renounce the religion of Ahura Mazda and worship me instead, and I shall give you a great gift, one as great as the one I gave to Zahhak, and you shall become the ruler of nations!"

Zarathustra replied, "Never will I worship you, O Evil One! Never shall I turn aside from the true religion of Ahura Mazda, even though I must die for it."

"Very well. Then tell me: How will you smite my demons? How will you strike down idolatry? What words will you use? What will be your weapons?"

"My weapons are the mortar, the cup, and the sacred haoma drink. And my words are the words of Ahura Mazda. With those weapons and words, I will strike you down and smite your demons, for it is Ahura Mazda that brought the world into being. With the Amesha Spentas, he brought it into existence."

Then Zarathustra sang the Ahura Vairya, and when he was done, he addressed Ahura Mazda, saying, "O great and good Ahura Mazda! Instruct me! Tell me how I may defeat the Angra Mainyu and all his demons. Tell me how I may keep the Nasu from defiling the house of your faithful people. Tell me how I may cleanse those people who have become unclean and make them pure again."

Ahura Mazda replied, "I shall tell you how you may do this, and it is done by invocations.

"Invoke my good and holy religion.

"Invoke the Blessed Immortals, the Amesha Spentas who rule the seven regions of the world.

"Invoke the firmament of Heaven, the limitless time, and Vayu, who is the holy wind.

"Invoke the wind, and Spenta Armaiti, who watches over the earth.

"Invoke my *fravashi*, my holy essence, the holy essence of Ahura Mazda, the greatest and most blessed of all beings.

"Invoke all of creation, which I, Ahura Mazda, have made."

Then Zarathustra replied, saying, "I invoke all the creation that Ahura Mazda has made.

"I invoke Mithras, the victorious one who is armed with great weapons.

"I invoke the holy Sarosh, who wields a club to smite the demons.

"I invoke the holy word of Ahura Mazda.

"I invoke the firmament of Heaven, the limitless time, and Vayu, who is the holy wind.

"I invoke the wind, and Spenta Armaiti, who watches over the earth.

"I invoke the good religion of Ahura Mazda, which is the one true religion.

Then Zarathustra asked, "O great and good Ahura Mazda, how shall I make the sacrifice? How shall I purify those who are unclean?"

Ahura Mazda then gave Zarathustra many good instructions for making the sacrifice and purifying those who are unclean, and when this was done, Zarathustra praised Ahura Mazda and made many invocations that drive away all that is evil.

When Angra Mainyu and the demons saw the holy sacrifice Zarathustra had made and heard his invocations, they became deranged and ran to and fro.

Angra Mainyu shouted to all the demons, "Come and gather! Gather at the gates of Hell!"

The demons all shouted, "Let us gather at the gates of Hell!" and ran there screaming, "The holy Zarathustra, son of Pourushaspa, is born! He is the sword that smites us! He is the bane of all that is evil! He deprives us of our worship!"

Thus, did the demons flee from the holy words and acts of Zarathustra.

The Creation of the World

In addition to the Zend-Avesta, Zoroastrian holy texts include the Bundahisn, a collection of religious writings in Middle Persian primarily having to do with cosmogony and cosmology. The Bundahishn was compiled in the ninth century and relates the history of creation and the battle between the good god Ohrmazd (Ahura Mazda) and the evil god Ahriman (Angra Mainyu). Two versions of the Bundahisn exist, the shorter Indian recension (or Lesser Bundahisn) and the longer Iranian recension (or Greater Bundahisn).

As part of his act of creation, Ohrmazd creates six Blessed Immortals, which are avatars or manifestations of various aspects of Ohrmazd himself and many other divine spirits who aid the work of Ohrmazd and the Blessed Immortals. Of course, Ahriman does the same—although the beings he creates all share in his evil nature. Ohrmazd also regulates the division of the year, month, and day at the time of his creation, and the act of creation is effected through the performance of the sacred Yazishn ceremony, a complex ritual still performed today in Zoroastrian fire temples.

The version of the creation presented here has been condensed from the original found in the Greater Bundahisn, *which contains a great deal of repetition and religious and philosophical commentary interwoven into the relation of the events of the creation and the strife between Ohrmazd and Ahriman.*

In the beginning, even before the existence of time, Ohrmazd lived in regions of light. Ohrmazd was omniscient and perfectly good, and the regions of light in the heavens were his abode. In the regions of darkness lived Ahriman, and he was evil and inclined to destruction. Both the regions of light and darkness were limitless, and between them was the Void.

Now, because Ohrmazd was omniscient, he knew of the existence of Ahriman, even though their two abodes were separated from one another. Ohrmazd knew that whatever he created, Ahriman would try to destroy it, and so he first created beings that existed only in a spiritual state, unable to move, unable to think, with bodies that were spiritual and not solid. These beings remained in this state for three thousand years.

Ahriman knew nothing of these beings until he rose out of his abyss and crossed the Void into the regions of light. Ahriman saw the light, and he hated it. He vowed to destroy it, but when he tried to attack the light, he discovered that it was braver and more powerful than he was. Therefore, Ahriman fled back into his regions of darkness, where he created the devs, evil beings that shared Ahriman's malice and desire to destroy. Ahriman mustered his army of devs and with them assailed the regions of light.

When Ohrmazd saw the beings that Ahriman had created, he was repulsed, finding them corrupt and putrid. But when Ahriman saw the beings Ohrmazd had created, he found them beautiful and delightful, and he coveted them for himself.

Ohrmazd then said to Ahriman, "O Evil One! Listen to me! If you aid the beings that I have made, and if you offer worship, I will give immortality to you and the beings you have created."

Ahriman replied, "These things I will not do. I will not aid the beings you have made. I will not offer worship. I set myself forever against you and your creation. Whatever you create, I will turn away from you. Whatever you create, I will convince it to love me instead."

"You cannot destroy me, O Evil One, for you are not omnipotent. You may hold sway over my creatures for a time, but in the end, they will all return to me." Then Ohrmazd thought to himself that unless he set a limit on the contest between himself and Ahriman, it would go on forever, and without that limit, Ahriman would further be able to corrupt whatever Ohrmazd had made and take it for his own.

Therefore, Ohrmazd said to Ahriman, "Let us agree to limit the period of our strife against one another to nine thousand years."

Because Ahriman could not see the outcome of the battle as Ohrmazd could, Ahriman said, "It is well. I agree."

Now, Ohrmazd knew that these nine thousand years would pass thusly: In the first three thousand, there would be peace, and his own will would hold sway; in the second three thousand, there would be a mingling of the wills of Ohrmazd and Ahriman; and in the third three thousand, Ahriman would be defeated, and the creatures of Ohrmazd would live in peace.

Then Ohrmazd uttered the Ahuna Vairya and showed Ahriman the progress of their strife and its eventual ending with the destruction of the devs and the triumph of Ohrmazd and his creation. So, it was that when the Evil One heard the words of the Ahuna Vairya, he fell to his knees and returned to his regions of darkness so weakened that he did not rise again for three thousand years.

In this time before the creation of the world, Ohrmazd was not Lord. It was only after he made the world that his lordship existed. Before all other things, Ohrmazd created the yazads, those spirits who are the essence of goodness and whose creation enhanced the body and the lordship of Ohrmazd. The next thing Ohrmazd created was time. This he did because he knew that without time to impose a limit, the depredations of Ahriman would continue forever. In creating time, Ohrmazd knew that he was also making it possible for Ahriman to do his own evil works, but that without time, there also would be no end to Ahriman's destructive acts. And the duration of time from Ohrmazd's creation of the world to the final defeat of the Evil One is a span of twelve thousand years, and when that span is over, Ohrmazd's creation will join him and live with him forever in his dwelling where time is limitless.

When Ohrmazd made his creatures, he formed them out of light, making them out of fire, which is light and bright and can be seen from far off. But when Ahriman made his creatures, he formed them out of darkness, making them sinful, corrupt, and misshapen. Ohrmazd also made spirits to aid him in his creation, spirits that are manifestations of Ohrmazd and are part of him. The first of these spirits was Vohuman (Good Thought). The first of Ahriman's creatures was Mitokht (Falsehood), and the second was Akoman (Evil Thought).

Now, while Ahriman remained insensate in his abyss, Ohrmazd made the physical world.

First, Ohrmazd made the sky. He made it out of steel and diamond, and its crown touched the regions of endless light. Next Ohrmazd created water, and that water helped him create the wind and rain. Ohrmazd drew the earth out of the water, and at first, it was flat and featureless, but out of the earth, Ohrmazd caused the mountains to grow, and placed within them metals, gems, stone, and other good things that may be found beneath the earth.

After Ohrmazd created the mountains, he made the first tree. This tree grew in the very center of the earth, and it had neither bark nor branch nor thorn. It was the parent of all plants and had the life force of all plants contained within it. Once the tree was created, Ohrmazd then made the good animals.

On the bank of the river Daiti that ran through the middle of the earth, Ohrmazd created the Gav, the Holy Bull. The Gav was three rods high at the shoulder and as white and shining as the full moon. The water and plants that Ohrmazd created he gave to the Gav so that he might have health and strength. Upon the other side of the river, Ohrmazd created Gayomard, the father of the human race, and to Gayomard Ohrmazd he gave the gift of sleep.

In the sky, Ohrmazd placed the Sun and the Moon. He also fixed the stars in the firmament and shaped them into constellations. He made the twelve that are the Ram, the Bull, the Twins, the Crab, the Lion, the Virgin, the Balance, the Scorpion, the Centaur, the Capricorn, the Water Bearer, the Fish, and many more. He made the stars of different brightnesses and divided the sky and the year into twelve portions.

When the time comes for the last battle with Ahriman, the stars will descend from the heavens and fight on the side of Ohrmazd. In between earth and sky, Ohrmazd made clouds and wind. From the clouds came rain, and also lightning.

When Ohrmazd created the world, he did so with the aid of six Blessed Immortals, and together with the most holy Ohrmazd, there are seven Blessed Immortals. Together with Ohrmazd, the Blessed Immortals do battle with evil forces, and the Blessed Immortals are both themselves and reflections of Ohrmazd.

The first of the Blessed Immortals is Ohrmazd himself, and for himself, he took the human beings of the world. The second Blessed Immortal is Vohuman, and for himself, he took all the good animals. Ardwahisht (Best Truth) is the third Blessed Immortal, and for himself, he took fire. The fourth Blessed Immortal is Shahrewar (Desirable Dominion), and for himself, he took metal. Spandarmad (Holy Devotion) is the fifth Blessed Immortal, and for herself, she took the earth. Hordad (Wholeness) is the sixth Blessed Immortal, and for herself, she took water. The seventh Blessed Immortal is Amurdad (Immortality), and for herself, she took the plants. With the aid of other divine spirits, the Blessed Immortals protect the world and keep it in existence.

According to the will of Ohrmazd, each day is divided into five segments: Morning, midday, evening, ablution time, and dawn. Each segment has a divine spirit to watch over it. Ohrmazd made these divisions because prior to the world's creation, all was illuminated by an eternal midday.

Ohrmazd created the world while performing the holy Yazishn ceremony with the Blessed Immortals. This he did in the Rapithwin Gah, the midday time of the day.

When the ceremony was over, and all had been created, Ohrmazd turned to the *farohars* of the human beings, the aspect of the soul that is always in the presence of Ohrmazd, and said, "I give you a choice:

You can assume a material form and thus strive against the Druj, the demon whose power is of corruption and death, so that you may conquer the Druj and thus enter into eternal life, perfect, deathless, and without an adversary. Or, do you want me to protect you forever from the forces of evil?"

The farohars knew that Ahriman and his demons would be conquered in the end, so they agreed to take on material bodies and thus live in the world Ohrmazd had made until the time came when they might regain their bodies and become perfect and immortal.

Now, when Ahriman became aware of the creations of Ohrmazd, he roused from his stupor, along with all the demons he had created, attacked first the sky, trying to pull it down and drag it under the earth, and all became as dark as night. Ahriman and his demons attacked the waters, sullying them and making them impure. He released upon the Earth all manner of vile creatures—dragons, serpents, toads, stinging insects, and many other kinds of venomous and noxious things so that no place on the Earth was free of them. Ahriman went to the first tree and poisoned it so that it withered and died. He went to the Gav and Gayomard and loosed upon them all manner of vices and suffering. This is how greed, poverty, disease, hunger, and other ills came into the world.

When Ohrmazd saw that Ahriman would attack the Gav, he gave him healing medicine to protect him and relieve his suffering. But even with that medicine, the Gav became feeble and died. To protect Gayomard, Ohrmazd cast him into a deep sleep, and when Gayomard awoke, he found the world plunged into the deepest darkness. The stars were at war with the demons, and all of creation was thrown into chaos.

Seeing the things that Ohrmazd had made now in disarray, Ahriman next attacked Gayomard. Ahriman sent Astwihad, the demon of death, and a thousand other demons to slay him, but no matter how they tried, they could not kill Gayomard, for the time of his death had not yet arrived.

Gayomard said, "Now that the Evil One has awakened and come to disturb the Earth, human beings shall arise from my seed and populate the world, and they shall do many good deeds."

Ahriman next went to the fire, sullying it with smoke and darkness. The planets and constellations fought with the demons of Ahriman, and for ninety days, the angels of Heaven fought with the demons of Ahriman, until finally Ahriman and all his minions were defeated and thrown into Hell, which is at the center of the world.

Part II: Bakhtiyar Nameh

Bakhtiyar Nameh *is a collection of stories compiled by Persian author Sams-al-Din Mohammad Daqayeqi Marvazi around the turn of the seventh century. The collection includes nine tales that are sandwiched within a frame story that tells the history of Prince Bakhtiyar, from his birth and abandonment by his royal parents to his eventual reunion with his family as a young adult. Thus, the frame story participates in the common folklore trope of the foundling prince, while the central stories each revolve around different topics.*

The frame story in Bakhtiyar Nameh *is set in the provinces of Sistan and Kirman. In ancient times, Sistan covered the region that now includes parts of Eastern Iran and Western Afghanistan on either side of the Helmand River, while Kirman is in South-central Iran. Tales involving Bakhtiyar's father, Azadbakht, also appear in the Arab collection known as* The Thousand and One Nights *or* The Arabian Nights.

The entire Bakhtiyar Nameh *is too long to be presented here in its entirety, so only the frame story and two of the internal tales are retold below.*

The Birth of Bakhtiyar

There was a time when the country of Sistan was ruled by a king named Azadbakht, who had a vizier named Sipehsalar. Sipehsalar was a man of great strength and skill. When he wielded his scimitar, even the Moon hid herself for fear of it.

Sipehsalar had a daughter, who was the most beautiful young woman in the whole kingdom, with jet-black hair perfumed with all the spices of Arabia. The most perfect red rose would look gray and wan next to Sipehsalar's daughter, who outshone all others as the noonday Sun does the Moon.

Sipehsalar loved his daughter excessively, to the point where he could not bear to be more than an hour without her. Now, there came a time when Sipehsalar had to go on a tour of inspection of the countryside, to see what state the kingdom was in and how her people were faring, and to ensure that the governors who ruled the various provinces were executing their offices justly. The journey dragged on and on, and soon Sipehsalar found himself becoming distraught over the amount of time he was spending away from his home and his family. Therefore, he summoned two messengers and sent them to his home to fetch his daughter and bring her to her father so that she might accompany him on the remainder of his journey.

The messengers rushed back to the capital city in haste. They went to Sipehsalar's house and told the young woman that her father desired that she join him as he toured the country. She assented to the request and, after packing the things that would be needful to her, got into the palanquin that had been readied to convey her to the place where her father was lodged.

It happened that while the messengers and Sipehsalar's daughter were on their way to meet her father, King Azadbakht was riding toward them on his way back to the city after having spent the day hunting.

When the king approached, the messengers dismounted their horses and prostrated themselves on the ground before him, saying, "May God save you, O king, and grant you a long and prosperous life."

"You are the messengers of Sipehsalar, yes? When you rejoin him, please give him my greetings and tell him I await with great interest the results of his inspection," said the king.

The messengers promised to do as the king bid them the moment they were again in Sipehsalar's presence.

The king then resumed his journey back home, but just as he passed the palanquin, a passing breeze lifted the curtain, revealing the lovely young woman seated inside. The king caught sight of Sipehsalar's daughter, and immediately his heart was inflamed with the most ardent love.

The king turned to the attendants who had accompanied him on the hunt and said, "Accompany this young woman back to the city, and see that she is lodged in the greatest comfort in my palace." Then Azadbakht said to the messengers, "I give you a new task: Return to Sipehsalar and tell him that I intend to make his daughter my wife and hope to be worthy of her and my father-in-law-to-be."

The Sipehsalar's messengers again prostrated themselves and said, "O great king, may God grant you a long life and riches beyond measure! May your throne be a light to the world, and your words ever wise! Sipehsalar surely will count himself the most fortunate of fathers. We ask that you allow us to conduct Sipehsalar's daughter to her father. There we will tell him your will so that he might have time to prepare for the wedding, as befits your royal majesty."

"What? Would you dare defy me? No, you shall go to Sipehsalar as I have commanded you, and I shall accompany his daughter back to the city myself." The king badly wanted to punish the messengers for their temerity, but he stayed his hand because he did not want Sipehsalar's daughter to think him cruel.

The messengers went on their way to bring the king's news to Sipehsalar, and the king and his retinue returned to the city with Sipehsalar's daughter, who was taken to the women's quarters, where she was received with great honor.

In the morning, King Azadbakht summoned all his chief advisers and the chief judges of his kingdom.

"I intend to marry the daughter of Vizier Sipehsalar, and I desire to know your thoughts on the matter," he said.

One and all, the advisers and judges told the king that it was a most auspicious match and preparations for the wedding should begin at once. To this end, they drew up a decree announcing the marriage and ceremonies that were to be held to solemnize it. The king then dictated a letter announcing his marriage and bid his secretaries make many copies that could be brought to all corners of his realm, so his people might know his happiness and rejoice with him. To Sipehsalar, the king wrote with his own hand, saying how honored he felt to have such a bride and hoping that Sipehsalar would bless the union and rejoice along with him.

When Sipehsalar received the king's letter, he felt anything but joy. Rather, he wept bitter tears to know that his beloved daughter would be taken from him and made the king's bride. Sipehsalar's tears were not just for sorrow; no, they were also tears of anger, for the king had not even had the decency to allow Sipehsalar's daughter to see her father one last time before being whisked away, nor had he had the decency to ask for the young woman's hand before publishing the marriage decree.

However, Sipehsalar had served the king for many years, and he was a man of wisdom and diplomacy. He wrote a response to the king that outwardly spoke of his gladness at having such a splendid son-in-law, and of his hope that the union would be a long and happy one, but in his heart, Sipehsalar was plotting revenge. There were many months yet left in his tour of inspection, and he vowed to use them well to sow seeds of distrust and sedition against the king and rally the powerful men of the kingdom to his own side.

Finally, Sipehsalar deemed his plans were ripe, and he summoned all the generals of the army to a council. First, he made the generals swear an oath of secrecy, and then he made sure that each of them would be willing to support whatever thing Sipehsalar told them needed to be done.

The generals took the oath and assured Sipehsalar of their loyalty, whereupon Sipehsalar said, "You have heard of the dastardly way King Azadbakht took my daughter to wife. He snatched her from the road like a brigand and rode back to the palace with her as though she were a piece of loot. What did I do to deserve this insult? I have only given him my loyal service from the very first day, but he rides off with my daughter without so much as a by-your-leave."

The generals all agreed that the king had used Sipehsalar very ill and asked what he required of them.

"Gather all your men. Arm them. And when all is ready, we attack Azadbakht and depose him like the cur he is," said Sipehsalar.

The Sipehsalar opened up his treasury and paid vast sums of money to the generals so that they might ready their armies for an assault on Azadbakht.

It took very little time to muster the army and march to Azadbakht's capital city, and even less time for the army to breach the walls and fan out through the streets, which they did in the dead of night.

Azadbakht was roused from sleep by the cries of those being slain and the clash of arms. He looked out the window and saw that his city was being attacked from all sides.

"What shall we do?" Azadbakht asked of his queen. "This army will have taken the city before dawn, and they will have my head on a pike at the gate soon thereafter."

"Let us fly as quickly as may be. Surely there is some other friendly prince who will welcome us in our time of need," said the queen.

Azadbakht agreed that this was the wisest course, and so he and the queen quickly prepared to travel to the kingdom of Kirman, whose ruler had always been on good terms with Azadbakht. The king ordered that horses be saddled. Then he put on his armor and girt on his sword before taking a great store of gems and gold from the treasury so that he and the queen might buy what was needful in their flight. Once the king and queen were mounted on their horses, they made their way to a secret underground passage that led out of the city and into the desert.

The king and queen traveled for the rest of the night and throughout the following day. They were weary and thirsty, but they went on until they arrived at a well that seemed to promise water. When the king drew some of the water, he found that it was brackish and foul and in no way fit to drink. But this was not the end of their troubles: The queen had been with child for the nine months prior, and the fear and hardship of their journey brought on her labor pains.

"My husband, leave this place and search for water. My pains are upon me, and it would not be meet for the king to die of thirst like a commoner if water were available nearby. My own life matters not. Save yourself, for you are the king," said the queen.

"That I will not do, for nothing in this world is dearer to me than my beloved wife. I would gladly set aside my throne and all my riches to keep you by my side. No, we stay together, for I do not know how I would live without you," said Azadbakht,

It was then that the queen cried out, and soon she gave birth to a baby boy. The child was exquisitely beautiful, surpassing even the Moon in the fairness of his features. The queen cradled him to her breast and began to nurse him as a mother should.

"My dearest wife, do not become attached to the child. We cannot take him with us. We have not enough food or water to support the three of us. We must leave him behind and hope that God will send good people to his aid, who will love him and raise him as their own," said the king.

The king then took his newborn son and wrapped him in a cloth that was richly embroidered with gold. He then put a bracelet made of ten large pearls about the child's neck. With hearts full of anguish, the king and queen mounted their horses and rode away, all the while commending their infant son to the care of the Almighty.

When Azadbakht and his queen arrived at the principal city of Kirman, the King of Kirman sent out musicians and servants to welcome his guests and conduct them in great honor to his palace. The King of Kirman commanded a great banquet to be held and sent his son and two other servants to wait upon Azadbakht and the queen, to see that they lacked for nothing.

The banquet was a splendid affair, with all manner of good food and good wine, and delightful music played by the palace musicians. Although Azadbakht was most grateful for the king's hospitality, nothing could assuage his grief over his son and the loss of his kingdom, and he could not hide his tears.

"Why do you weep, O my guest, who is most welcome of all to my house? Behold, here is a feast in your honor and music to delight you. What reason have you to mourn?" asked the King of Kirman.

"O my most royal host, truly your hospitality is without stint and compare. But I cannot rejoice when my kingdom has been taken from me, and an enemy sits upon my throne," said Azadbakht.

The King of Kirman then bade Azadbakht tell his whole tale, and when the king had heard all, he felt deep compassion toward his guest. He ordered his musicians and servants to divert Azadbakht and his queen all day, to help keep their minds from their sorrows.

In the morning, he mustered his army.

The King of Kirman said to Azadbakht, "Behold, O my most royal guest, I have mustered my army for you. I bid you lead it to your capital, and so depose the usurper to your throne."

Azadbakht thanked the King of Kirman most gratefully and then led the army back to Sistan.

When Sipehsalar saw Azadbakht approaching at the head of a mighty army, he fled in fear, while the people of Sistan bowed down before Azadbakht and begged his forgiveness and mercy.

Azadbakht pardoned them, one and all, and ascended his throne, from where he ruled with great justice and mercy. He paid the King of Kirman's soldiers most generously and then sent them back to Kirman, laden with many precious gifts to give their king.

The kingdom of Sistan was peaceful and prosperous under Azadbakht's rule, but the king and the queen could never forget their tiny son, whom they had abandoned at that lonely well in the desert. Both of them were convinced that he must have been devoured by wild beasts soon after they left him, and for all the success of Azadbakht's reign, their hearts were ever heavy and in mourning for their dear son.

Bakhtiyar and the Bandits

Little did Azadbakht and his queen know that not long after they had ridden away from the well, a band of robbers rode up, having heard the wails of the infant. The robbers' leader was named Firokh Suvar, and when he picked up the crying child, he was taken by the infant's great beauty.

"Look at this child," he said to his followers. "Surely, he is the son of some great and powerful person. See how beautiful he is? And look, he is wrapped in a cloth of gold, and has a bracelet of ten pearls around his neck."

"What will you do with him?" asked one of the robbers.

"I will keep him and raise him as my own. I have no child, and I have longed for one. We will take him with us, and we will call him Khodadad."

Firokh took the infant to his home, where he found a wet nurse to tend him. The boy grew and flourished under the care of Firokh and the nurse, and when he was old enough, Firokh taught him all the things a man ought to know, such as horsemanship and the wielding of arms. So strong and clever was the boy that by the time he was fifteen years old, even an army of five hundred men could not stand against him.

Firokh loved Khodadad very deeply and took the boy with him everywhere he went. However, Khodadad refused to help his father and his band of robbers to plunder a caravan. Khodadad felt sorry for the people of the caravan, and he found banditry distasteful. Firokh agreed that Khodadad need not participate in the attack but insisted that he go along and wait nearby until the looting was done.

One day, Firokh led his band out to attack a nearby caravan, and, as was usual, Khodadad went with them but waited to the side while the bandits did their work. However, this time, Firokh and his band were outnumbered, and the men of the caravan fought back with such ferocity that many of the robbers were killed and many others were taken prisoner. During the battle, Firokh was wounded and was just about to be taken prisoner when Khodadad came charging in to his rescue. Khodadad fought bravely and was near to rescuing Firokh when he fell from his horse and was taken prisoner himself. Khodadad, Firokh, and the other robbers who had been captured were put into chains and marched to the capital city of Sistan, where they were brought before King Azadbakht for judgment.

Now, when Azadbakht looked upon Khodadad, his heart welled up with love, for he thought, *Surely the infant I abandoned at the well would be a youth such as this, were he still alive!*

Then Azadbakht said to Khodadad, "Step forward and tell me your name."

"O most royal sovereign, my name is Khodadad."

"Why is it that a youth with such strength and beauty as yours should plunder a caravan and steal things belonging to others, things to which you have no right?"

Khodadad replied, "O most royal sovereign, it is true that I was there, but it is false that I stole anything from anyone, and God himself sees my innocence."

Azadbakht pardoned Khodadad then and there and ordered that his chains be removed.

Then he gave the boy his own cloak and said, "No more shall you be called Khodadad. From today forth, you shall be known as Bakhtiyar, and fortune shall be your friend from henceforth."

Then Azadbakht said to the captured robbers, "I grant you pardon on two conditions. One is that you never again engage in banditry. The other is that you enter into my service. If you do both those things, you will be rewarded generously."

The robbers agreed, and from that time forward, they served the king, and caravans passed through the country of Sistan unmolested.

Azadbakht put Bakhtiyar in charge of the royal stables, and so well did the youth discharge his duties that soon all the horses were sleek and fat. When the king asked how his horses had prospered so well, he was told that Bakhtiyar's attendance upon them was the reason.

Azadbakht then sent for Bakhtiyar and said, "You have managed my stables so very well that I think you might be entrusted with something of greater importance. Here are the keys to my treasury. You are now the keeper of my treasure."

Bakhtiyar prostrated himself before Azadbakht and promised to do his utmost to discharge his duties with honesty and discretion.

In managing the king's treasury, Bakhtiyar proved himself to be just as adept at keeping the horses. Azadbakht soon came to rely on the young man's good advice, and in time, the king would not hold audiences with any person unless Bakhtiyar could be there to advise him.

The Ten Viziers

Now, Azadbakht also had ten viziers who served him. These viziers had seen the rise of Bakhtiyar in the king's esteem, and they burned with envy. Therefore, they held counsel together and agreed that they would look for an opportunity to accomplish Bakhtiyar's fall from favor, and even his death, if at all possible.

The viziers watched and waited, and finally, their patience was rewarded when one night, Bakhtiyar spent the night drinking in the treasury. He drank so much wine that he was nearly insensible, and when he exited the treasury with the intent of going to his quarters, he instead became lost and wandered through the palace until he arrived at the king's bedchamber. Bakhtiyar opened the door and saw a sort of throne, and many cushions and hangings of silk in a room lit by many candles. Seeing only a comfortable room, and feeling the wine's effects, Bakhtiyar went inside, sat down upon the throne, and promptly fell asleep. Some time later, Azadbakht entered the chamber, thinking to take his rest. He was furious to find Bakhtiyar sitting on his chair, fast asleep.

"How dare you enter my private apartments! Explain yourself at once!" shouted the king.

Bakhtiyar was still heavily intoxicated, so the only effect the king's shouts had was to rouse Bakhtiyar from sleep enough that he fell off the chair. But even then, he was too insensible to realize his peril; instead, he simply rolled underneath the throne and went back to sleep.

Azadbakht then called for servants to remove Bakhtiyar, put him in chains, and throw him into the dungeon. The king then drew his sword and strode into the women's quarters, where he demanded that the queen explain how Bakhtiyar was found in the royal bedchamber.

"O my king and O my husband, I have no knowledge of this," said the queen.

"Spare me your lies. There is no way he could have found his way into that chamber without your help."

"O my king, I say to you that I have no knowledge of this, and if you wish proof of my innocence, keep me confined here until you can establish the truth of the matter."

In the morning, Azadbakht summoned the ten viziers. He told them what had transpired the night before and asked their advice on what should be done.

One vizier realized that this was the chance he and his fellows had waited for, and so he said, "What did you expect, O my king and O my royal master, when you brought into your service a low-born churl who furthermore had been raised by brigands? I had my doubts about him from the first but held my tongue because your glorious majesty seemed so taken with the boy. But now his true nature has manifested itself, and you must punish him accordingly."

Azadbakht then commanded that Bakhtiyar be brought before him.

When the young man was stood before the king in his chains, Azadbakht said, "What have you to say for yourself? I, for one, think you the most ungrateful wretch in my entire kingdom. I raised you to high office and entrusted you with vital duties, but in the end, you betrayed me by sneaking into my private apartments. Speak! Explain yourself!"

"O my king and O my royal master, I truly am grateful for all that you have given me, and all I have to say for myself is that I have no memory of how I arrived in your apartments. I beg your majesty's forgiveness and mercy for what I did since I knew not what I was doing and meant no harm," said Bakhtiyar.

Then the first vizier requested the king's permission to go to the women's quarters and inquire as to what the queen knew of these events, and Azadbakht gave his assent.

The vizier went before the queen and said, "O my queen, you surely know of the entrance of Bakhtiyar into the royal chambers last night, and you surely know that the king accuses you of having given him entrance. His majesty is greatly wroth with you, and the only way that you can save yourself from his vengeance is to tell him that Bakhtiyar entered the royal quarters with the intent to ravish you and with the intent to do away with the king and steal his throne. If you say this, the king will have mercy on you and execute Bakhtiyar for his crimes. It is the only way to save yourself."

The queen was astonished at this advice and said, "How can I say that when I know it not to be true? I will not be the cause of an innocent man's death."

"Bakhtiyar is not an innocent man, my lady. Before he rose in the king's favor, he was a brigand among brigands, and your statement will merely restore to him the fate that should have been his long ago."

The vizier made these and many other arguments until finally, the queen gave in and agreed to testify against Bakhtiyar with the words the vizier told her to say.

After hearing the queen's testimony, the king ordered that Bakhtiyar be returned to the prison in chains, where he was to await the most terrifying punishment the king could bestow upon him. Bakhtiyar was duly thrown into the dungeon, and the viziers went to their homes rejoicing that their time of vengeance had come at last and thinking of ways they might induce the king to execute the young man sooner rather than later.

Bakhtiyar's First Story: The Tale of the Unfortunate Merchant

On the following day, the second vizier stood before the king and said, "O most gracious majesty, may you have a long life, and may your reign shine forever! I have come to ask you to execute Bakhtiyar without delay since it is vital that your majesty not be seen as weak and vacillating."

"Very well. But first, have him brought here so that I may tell him his fate," said the king.

Accordingly, Bakhtiyar was taken from the prison and soon stood before the king in his chains.

"You are here so that I may pronounce sentence upon you, for it is my wish that your death be made an example for all others who might harbor ill thoughts against me or my household," said Azadbakht.

"O mighty sovereign, may God grant you long life and limitless victories over your enemies. I know it to be my duty to try and save myself from the gallows since I know myself to be innocent, and since God knows this also. But unfortunately, I share the plight of the merchant who was ceaselessly plagued by misfortune, such that everything he attempted went awry," said Bakhtiyar.

"I do not know this tale. Tell it to me now."

"As your majesty wishes. Here is the tale . . . A merchant once lived in the city of Basrah, and this merchant was immensely wealthy. But no matter what business or trade he attempted, it invariably came to naught. Because of this, it did not take long before all his wealth was sorely depleted, and he was on the verge of ruin.

"When the merchant saw how little of his money was left, he decided to invest it in a store of grain, which he intended to keep until the following year so that he might sell it at a profit. He duly bought the grain and stored it in a granary, but the following year, the harvest was better than usual, and as a result, the price of grain fell. Therefore, the merchant decided to keep his grain in storage and wait to see what the following year might bring. But that winter, there was so much rain that the city flooded, including the storehouse where the merchant kept his grain, and so the grain rotted and had to be thrown away.

"After some time spent mourning this misfortune, the merchant decided to sell his house and join a company of merchants, who were sailing to a far land in hopes of finding fortune there. But on the journey, a storm blew up and wrecked the ship. Many of those aboard drowned, but the merchant was among those lucky few who managed to cling to a plank and drifted onto land.

"Hungry and thirsty, his clothes in tatters, the merchant wandered inland. He had walked some miles through a desert when he saw a man in the distance. The merchant's spirits rose, for where one man was, others might be, and perhaps there would be someone who could help him. So, the merchant walked toward the man and soon saw that there was a village nearby. The chief of the village, or dikhan, had made himself a little summer house just outside the village, and he happened to be there when the merchant arrived, and so saw the poor, tattered wretch. The dikhan then told his servants to fetch the man and bring him into the summer house, where the dikhan inquired as to what had happened to the merchant and made him comfortable with food and drink. The dikhan was so moved by the merchant's tale of woe that he gave the merchant some of his clothes and bid him stay as his guest until his fortunes could be reversed.

"The dikhan placed the merchant in charge of his fields of grain, saying that when the harvest came in, the merchant might have an eleventh share of it to be his. The merchant was pleased and grateful and worked diligently to see that the crops were properly tended. All his diligence paid off, for when the harvest came in, it proved more than usually abundant.

"The merchant did an accounting of the harvest and discovered that the share promised to him by the dikhan was quite substantial.

Surely, he never meant to give me this much, thought the merchant. *What if he chooses not to keep his word?*

Therefore, the merchant took an eleventh share of the grain and hid it away, thinking to restore it to the dikhan if he indeed kept his promise. The merchant hid that eleventh share of grain in a nearby cave, but it was discovered by a thief, who stole it all away.

"When the dikhan made his accounting of the harvest, he set aside an eleventh share for the use of the merchant. The merchant then confessed that he had doubted the dikhan's honesty and had already hidden an eleventh share in a cave. The dikhan duly sent some of his servants to recover that store of grain, but when they got to the cave, they found that it had disappeared. They returned in haste to the dikhan and told him what they had seen, whereupon the dikhan turned to the merchant and said, 'Ungrateful wretch! Not only would you doubt my word after all my help, but you would lose me a full eleventh share of a fine harvest! Begone! You leave as you came, with nothing. Do not return to my village ever again.'

"The merchant left the village and headed toward the seashore, mourning his misfortune and wondering how he might save himself. When he arrived at the shore, he came across six men from the village who were pearl divers. The merchant and the men knew one another, and when the divers asked why the merchant was so downcast, he told them his whole sorry tale.

"'Oh, that is so unfortunate,' said one of the divers. 'We surely must help you. We will bring you whatever we find the next time we dive for pearls, to restore your fortunes.'

"And so, the divers accordingly dove into the water, and each one brought up a beautiful pearl and gave it to the merchant. The merchant was most grateful, and he went on his way with a merry heart, thinking of all the ways he might use the pearls to increase his fortune.

"Along the road, the merchant was soon overtaken by a band of robbers, who happened to be going the same direction. Desiring not to lose what little fortune he now had, the merchant put three of the pearls into his mouth and concealed the rest among his clothing. At first, the robbers did not bother the merchant, but at one point, he decided to speak to them, and one of the pearls came out of his mouth. When the robbers saw this, they threatened the merchant with great violence if he did not give him the rest. The merchant accordingly gave them the other two pearls in his mouth but kept the rest concealed. Placated, the robbers went on their way, and the merchant thanked the Almighty that at least he still had half his treasure to do with as he would.

"The merchant continued on his journey, but because he could not afford a room in an inn, he was forced to sleep in a nearby barn. This, combined with his long journey on the road, had disarranged and dirtied his clothing so that when he arrived at the shop of the jeweler, where he intended to sell the pearls, the jeweler looked askance at him. The merchant brought out the pearls that he wished to sell and asked what the jeweler might be willing to pay. The jeweler was astonished that such large magnificent pearls would be in the possession of such a rag-tag person as the merchant.

"'How did you come by these pearls?' asked the jeweler.

"'My friends gave them to me as a parting gift,' said the merchant.

"'A likely story. Perhaps you stole them from my shop and are now trying to swindle me.'

"'Most assuredly, I am telling the truth.'

But the jeweler would not believe him, no matter how much the merchant protested, and soon the two men were engaged in a violent squabble that drew the attention of others in the marketplace. The jeweler was a man of some repute in the town, and so his story was believed over that of the merchant. Word of the argument came to the king, who pronounced the merchant guilty. The pearls were given to the jeweler, and the merchant was taken away to prison to await sentencing.

"Now, it happened that a few days after the merchant was imprisoned, the divers who had given him the pearls came to the city. They decided to go to the prison to distribute alms, and there they found their friend, bound in chains. When they asked the merchant what had happened, he related the whole sad tale. The pearl divers were outraged and went immediately to the king's court, where they explained the situation and vouched for the merchant's innocence, with the result that the merchant was freed and the jeweler brought before the king to explain himself. When the jeweler could offer no defense for his actions, the king pronounced him guilty and executed him for bringing false witness against a stranger. The king then turned the jeweler's shop and other property over to the merchant to be his in recompense for what he had unjustly suffered. He then ordered the merchant to be given a fine set of clothes and a hot bath and made the merchant the overseer of the royal treasury.

"The merchant served the king most diligently and was rewarded accordingly. This roused the envy of one of the king's viziers, who began to look for a means by which he might cause the merchant's downfall.

"Now, the king's daughter had a summer house next to the treasury, where she would spend a few days from time to time as it pleased her. A mouse had made a hole in the wall that divided the treasury from the summer house's grounds. One day, the merchant needed to drive a nail into the wall, and he, unfortunately, hit upon the mouse's nest, such that when the nail went into the wall, it went quite through and knocked out one of the bricks on the summer house side, creating a good-sized hole. The merchant saw what had happened and blocked up the hole with some clay.

"The vizier happened to see the merchant applying the clay to the wall and decided that this was his chance to rid himself of his rival. He accordingly went to the king and said that he had seen the merchant drive a nail into the wall and knock out a brick on the other side so that he could spy on the king's daughter and that the merchant had stoppered the hole with clay in an attempt to conceal his crime. The king was outraged at this and stormed down to the treasury, where he saw the merchant with dirty hands, having just finished applying the last of the wet clay.

"The king believed what the vizier said, despite the merchant's protestations of innocence and his explanation of what had actually happened. The king then ordered the merchant's eyes to be scooped out and his person to be set outside the palace gate. The king then went to the summer house to see to his daughter's welfare, only to be told that she had not been there for some days since she had decided to spend her time in another part of the palace. After hearing this, the king went to the treasury and removed the clay from the hole, which he saw had indeed been the work of a mouse. He also saw that the brick had been dislodged by accident and that the merchant had been both honest and trustworthy. The king, therefore, ordered the vizier to be severely punished and deeply lamented and regretted that he had not taken the time to investigate before ordering the merchant's fate.

"Therefore, your majesty," said Bakhtiyar, having completed his tale, "we see how the king might have prevented both his distress and that of the merchant had he but taken the time to understand what had truly happened, and not made a judgment in anger. If your majesty pleases, be not hasty in your judgment, to avoid the fate of that king. Give me some more time to prove my innocence."

Azadbakht was impressed by Bakhtiyar's story and duly agreed to give him another day's respite. He ordered that Bakhtiyar be taken back to prison and postponed the execution for the time being.

Bakhtiyar's Last Story: The Tale of the King of Persia

Day after day, Bakhtiyar was brought before the king, and each day one of the viziers, in turn, would make the case for Bakhtiyar's execution. But day after day, Bakhtiyar begged mercy of the king and won a stay of execution by telling the king a lively tale.

This went on for nine days, and on the tenth day, the tenth vizier sent a message to the queen that said, "O my queen, well you know that the brigand Bakhtiyar has been sentenced to death, but every day he manages to gain himself time by means of tales. I implore you to speak to your royal husband and demand that this farce is put to an end and the criminal executed without delay."

The queen did as the vizier asked. She spoke to the king before he left the royal apartments, and with his wife's persuasion, he agreed that today indeed, Bakhtiyar would meet his end. The king then went into the council chamber, where the viziers were already waiting for him.

Before the tenth vizier could rise to make his case, the king said, "I have decided that we must put an end to this farce. Today Bakhtiyar will be executed."

Then the king commanded that Bakhtiyar be brought into the chamber, and when he arrived, the king said, "For nine days now you have protested your innocence, but we have seen not one bit of evidence that you are telling the truth. Today indeed shall you be executed, for I have made the decree."

Bakhtiyar began to weep when he heard this and said, "I know that I am innocent, and have used my tales as a way to gain myself time in the hopes that somehow I might escape this fate. But now I see that this fate is indeed what God has in store for me, and I will not fight against my destiny as did the King of Persia, for I have no more hope of success than did he."

Azadbakht said, "I have not heard this tale of the King of Persia. I bid you tell it to me."

"As your most gracious majesty commands. Here is my tale: Once there was a King of Persia, who was mighty and wealthy, but he was unhappy because he had no child. He prayed and prayed that God might give him a son, and at length, one of the women of his household was found with child. The king was overjoyed that, at last, he might have a son and an heir, but that night he had a strange dream. In the dream, an old man said to him, 'God has given you a son, but his life will be short and his end tragic. When the child reaches his seventh year, a lion shall seize him and carry him to the top of a mountain, then throw him down the side, and the child shall roll to the bottom all covered in blood and earth.'

"The king was much troubled by this dream and asked his wisest viziers what it meant and what might be done about it, but all they could say was, 'If this is the fate God has decreed, then who are you to think it might be turned aside?' The king would not be dissuaded and said that he would indeed struggle against this fate even if it were the Almighty himself who decreed it.

"Some days later, one of the king's viziers drew up a horoscope for the king in which he saw that the king would be killed by his own son twenty years hence. The vizier went to the king to inform him of what he had found, and the king said, 'If you have spoken falsehood, you shall forfeit your life.'

"In the meantime, the king ordered that an underground chamber be constructed to hold his son and the boy's nurse, as proof against the doom predicted by the dream. The nurse and the child lived there for seven years, and at the end of the seventh year, a lion found its way into the chamber, where it devoured the nurse and then snatched up the child. The lion brought the child to the top of a mountain and then released him, whereupon the child rolled to the bottom, where he lay half-dead, covered in blood and earth.

"Not long thereafter, one of the king's secretaries happened to ride by that place and found the child, who was badly wounded but still alive. The secretary took the child into his home, where he treated the boy like one of his own children and taught him his trade. Meanwhile, the king had gone to the underground chamber to see whether his dream had come true. Finding the chamber deserted, he assumed that the nurse had run away with the child, and so he ordered messengers to go throughout the land to find her and the child, but they always returned without success.

"Time passed, and soon the king's son had attained the age of thirteen years, at which time his foster father determined that he was sufficiently schooled and trustworthy to accompany him to his employment within the palace. The king often saw the secretary and his young assistant, and each time he looked upon the youth, he felt an increase in his affection for the lad, until one day he told the secretary that he would like to take the boy into his service. The secretary assented with many thanks since serving the king was a great honor not usually accorded to one so young. To the young man, the king gave the office of armor-bearer and the duty to attend upon the king's person.

"The young man served his king with great distinction for many years, until one day the kingdom of Persia was beset by an enemy, who had mustered a powerful army and marched upon the capital with the intent of sacking it and taking the throne away from the king. The King of Persia gathered his troops and went to the field to meet the foe, and, of course, the young armor-bearer went in the king's train. A fierce battle ensued. Soon, the combatants were all so smeared with blood and dust that no man could tell friend from foe. The young armor-bearer was in the thick of the fray and, thinking himself among the enemy, laid blow upon blow on any man who came near him. Unfortunately, one of his blows landed upon his sovereign, severing his arm from his body.

"The king recognized his armor-bearer as the one who had dealt him the blow, and with many imprecations against him, quit the field, for his injury was so severe there was no way he could continue the fight. When the Persian army saw their king withdraw from the battle grievously wounded, they fell into disarray, and the field was lost. The king sued for peace, and a truce was reached with the enemy ruler upon payment of an extortionate sum of money. The armor-bearer was clapped in irons and thrown into prison, with none of his protestations of innocence given any heed.

"The king was taken on a litter back to his apartments, where he was tended by the best physicians in the land, both day and night. However, all their efforts were in vain. The wound festered, and soon it became apparent that the king had not much longer to live. The king, therefore, summoned the vizier who had foretold his death and said to him, 'You prophesied that I would be killed by my own son when he reached his twentieth year, but you see that I have not. I have been mortally wounded by my armor-bearer, the son of one of the palace secretaries. Your life, therefore, is forfeit, for your prophecy was false.'

"The vizier replied, 'It may be as your illustrious majesty says, but first we should have the armor-bearer brought here so that we might ask him about his origins. Your majesty doubtless would not want to execute an innocent man.'

"The king agreed that this course was just, and so the armor-bearer was taken from prison and brought before the king and the vizier. 'Tell me,' said the king to the young man, 'where are you from and who are your parents?'

"'I know not the country of my origin and I know not my parents, save that I was told that my father was a king. When I was but an infant, my nurse and I were lodged in an underground chamber. When I attained the age of seven years, a lion forced his way into our dwelling, where he savaged and devoured my nurse and then carried me up to the top of a mountain. There the lion loosed his grip, and I tumbled down to the foot of the mountain. That is where the secretary found me. He took me into his home and raised me as his own son until your majesty took me into your service.'

"The King of Persia then recognized the armor-bearer as his own son, and so handed to him his throne, and made the vizier the prime minister of the land. Three days later, the king died from his wounds."

Having concluded his tale, Bakhtiyar said to King Azadbakht, "This is why, O glorious king, I said that I was like the King of Persia, for though I might struggle against the dictates of Heaven, I must go to the fate that awaits me, whether I will it or not."

The Fate of Bakhtiyar

Azadbakht was moved by the young man's story and ordered the guards to take him back to his prison cell. Upon hearing this, the viziers all stood up and protested, saying they would resign their posts and leave the country if the execution was not held forthwith.

"Very well. The execution may go forward. But I, for one, will not witness it—my heart could not bear to see this young man put to death. You must take him and do the deed yourselves," said Azadbakht.

The viziers then proclaimed that Bakhtiyar was to be executed in the public square at midday. They had the gallows prepared in the main square and ordered the people to witness the event.

Now, it happened that Firokh Suvar, Bakhtiyar's foster father, had come to the city with some of his companions on business of his own that day, and he was wearing the golden cloak in which he had found the infant at the side of the well. Firokh saw the crowds assembling and the gallows prepared. He did not wish to watch the execution, so he began to resume his journey to where he intended to do business. Just then, the crowd parted to let the guards come through with the prisoner, and Firokh recognized his dear son weighed down with many chains.

Firokh and his friends rushed to the young man's aid, and after wresting him away from the guards, Firokh made loud demands to have an audience with the king.

When he was brought before Azadbakht, Firokh said, "I beg of your most illustrious majesty not to kill this young man! This is my beloved son, a man of good heart, and I know that he must be innocent of any crime of which he has been accused. If you must have blood, take mine as well, for I cannot live without him."

"Your wish certainly can be granted," said Azadbakht.

"O my king, you know not what foolishness this is! Surely this youth is the son of a mighty king and queen. Think of what they would do if they found that you had killed their child!"

"First, you protested that he is your son, but now you say he is someone else's. Tell the truth, or I really shall have you executed along with him."

"I am telling the truth, O my king and O the delight of the world. I found my son at the edge of a well in the desert, an infant wrapped in the very cloak I am wearing now. And around his neck was a bracelet of ten pearls, which I carry with me to this day."

Firokh took out the bracelet of pearls and showed them to Azadbakht, who recognized them and the cloak as the things he and his queen had left with their infant son when they had abandoned him in the wilderness. He then asked Firokh to give him the cloak and the pearls, whereupon he took them to the queen and showed them to her.

"Why these are the cloak and pearls we left with our dear son! How did you come upon them? Does our son yet live? Tell me!" she said.

"I shall do better than tell you. I shall bring him here in the flesh."

The king then sent servants to fetch Bakhtiyar. When Bakhtiyar arrived, Azadbakht struck off his chains and put a royal turban on his head. Then he wrapped the young man in a royal cloak and conducted him to the queen.

"This is our son, O my wife, who we left at the well," said Azadbakht.

When the queen heard this, milk sprang from her breasts.

The king and the queen embraced Bakhtiyar with great joy and many tears of happiness.

Then the king said to the queen, "Tell me, why did you propose to destroy this young man with false testimony?"

"Your viziers came to me and told me that your anger against me would be boundless were I not to confess what they told me to confess. I resisted as long as I could, but in the end, I had to give in to them," said the queen.

At this, Azadbakht fell into a rage. He ordered the immediate execution of all ten viziers, who died that very day on the gallows they had prepared for Bakhtiyar. Azadbakht then turned over his kingdom to Bakhtiyar, who made Firokh Suvar his chief vizier and gave positions of authority to Firokh's companions. The people all rejoiced that Azadbakht and his queen had been reunited with their son, and they pledged their fidelity and love for their new ruler. Bakhtiyar had a long and prosperous reign, and ever did he rule over his people with wisdom and justice.

Part III: Tales from the Shahnameh

The Tale of Kayumars and Hushang

The first few stories in the Shahnameh are tales of ancient and likely mythical kings. The one retold below is set in a mythical past when human beings could still communicate directly with animals, birds, and supernatural creatures such as fairies. As is common with such stories, the earliest kings are credited with discovering or inventing things that are basic to human survival, such as clothing and fire. Here we learn of the discovery of fire and of the origin of the festival of Sadeh, which still takes place every year today, fifty days before No-Ruz, the Iranian New Year, which is celebrated on the vernal equinox. As a midwinter festival, Sadeh celebrates fire's ability to defeat the cold and looks forward to the spring that is yet to come.

The very first king of Persia was a man named Kayumars. He wore clothing made of leopard skins, and so did his people, for other forms of clothing had not yet been made. It was Kayumars who first learned how to make clothing and prepare food, and he taught these things to the people. Kayumars was tall and strong, and the glory of his power shone out from him so that all bowed down before his presence, even the animals, both wild and tame.

Kayumars had one son, whose name was Siamak. Siamak was fair of face and very wise. Kayumars loved Siamak more than anything else in the world, and Siamak was the source of all Kayumars's joy.

Now, Siamak had no enemies among the people, for he was wise and just. However, Ahriman looked upon him and greatly envied him, and so vowed to destroy him. Ahriman went to his own son, a demon who hungered for destruction as a wolf hungered for prey, and told him to gather an army and attack Kayumars's kingdom so that it might be destroyed, and to kill Siamak.

Ahriman made his plans in secret, so Kayumars knew nothing of the danger he was in. But the angel Sorush appeared to Siamak in a dream, warning him of the approaching army. Siamak was enraged by this and mustered an army of his own. Siamak and his soldiers went to war clad only in leopard skins, for armor was yet to be invented. When Siamak and his army arrived at the place where Ahriman's son had arrayed his own soldiers, Siamak rushed forward to attack Ahriman's demon son. The battle did not last long; the demon took his long, sharp claws and drove them into Siamak's body, killing him.

When Kayumars heard that Siamak was dead, he fell into deep grief. He wept and tore at his beard, and all his kingdom wept with him, for Siamak had been much loved. The army arrayed itself before Kayumars and sent up a shout of grief. All the people dressed in blue to show that they, too, mourned Siamak. Even the animals and birds grieved for the death of that noble young man.

The entire kingdom mourned for one year, and then one night, Sorush appeared to Kayumars in a dream.

Sorush said, "Grieve no more. The time of your vengeance is near. If you muster your army and march out against the demon, you will have your revenge."

Now, Siamak himself had a son, a noble young man named Hushang. No one could match Hushang for intelligence or courtliness, and Kayumars relied on Hushang's good counsel and bravery.

Kayumars said to Hushang, "The time of our vengeance has come. Muster an army and lead it forth. I would lead it myself, but I am an old man now, so that duty must fall to you."

Hushang did as his grandfather bid him. He assembled a great army of fairies and all manner of savage beasts, and birds, cattle, and sheep. The army rode out with Hushang in the lead and Kayumars in the rear. Soon they met the army of demons, and a fierce battle took place. This time the demons were no match for Hushang's army. The lions, tigers, and other fierce beasts tore the demon soldiers to shreds, and Siamak himself met the demon who had killed his father and clove him in two. Then, he cut the demon's head off and flayed the skin off his body.

Having avenged his son, Kayumars died, and Hushang took over the throne. Hushang ruled justly and wisely, and his kingdom prospered under his rule.

One day, Hushang rode into the mountains with some companions. Suddenly a great black dragon appeared before them. It had blood-red eyes, and smoke and flame issued from its gaping mouth. Hushang picked up a rock and flung it at the beast. The beast dodged the rock and then went away, but this was not the end of the adventure; when the rock struck the stones that stood behind the dragon, a great shower of sparks went up. This is how Hushang discovered that flint might be used to make fire and how the people first learned to make and use fire. Hushang deemed this a great gift from God, and from that day forth, the people always prayed to God facing a fire.

That night, Hushang and his friends made a great bonfire and held a feast. They danced around the fire, celebrating and drinking wine, and this is how the feast of Sadeh came to be.

Now that Hushang knew how to make fire, he then set out to see what other things might come from the rocks around him. He took some ore and smelted it, and in this way, he discovered iron. Then he took the iron and made many useful things, such as hatchets, maces, and saws. Next, Hushang looked for a way to bring more water into his kingdom. He dug channels to bring water into the fields and thus invented irrigation. Once the people had a good source of water, they could plant more crops and grow more grain and fruit, and thus Hushang's kingdom prospered greatly.

Hushang also decreed which animals were to be domesticated and which were to remain wild. He decreed which animals could be hunted and which were to serve the people. He learned how to catch and flay fur-bearing animals like squirrels and ermine and turn their pelts into warm clothing.

Hushang worked tirelessly to better his kingdom and make it more prosperous. He dispensed justice and ruled with wisdom. However, for all his wisdom, Hushang was still a mortal man, and at the end of his days, he perished, as must we all.

Jamshid the Magnificent

Kayumars and Hushang may have benefited humanity through their discoveries of fire, metalworking, and clothing, but their accomplishments pale compared to those of Jamshid. Jamshid builds on discovering metalworking by inventing armor for both men and horses, discovering how to spin and weave fibers into thread and cloth and how to dye those materials, and create a social order within his kingdom.

Unfortunately, Jamshid falls victim to the sin of pride, thinking that his success as king makes his glory rival even that of God. Jamshid learns a hard lesson about this when his kingdom is captured by Zahhak, a neighboring prince who has been corrupted by Iblis. In the character of Iblis, the Muslim devil, we see Islam as part of the Persian culture that Ferdowsi knew, even though the story is set in a time before the advent of Islam.

The Reign of Jamshid

Jamshid was the son of King Tahmures and was determined to be a good king like his father, and indeed the whole world submitted to Jamshid's royal power. Not only did the people acknowledge him as king, but so did the birds and animals, and even the demons and fairies bowed before him.

Of himself, Jamshid said, "I am king, and I am priest. The grace of God is mine, and it shines forth from me. I will put down the evildoers, and the soul of the people I will guide toward the light."

The first thing Jamshid did upon assuming the throne was turn his thought to his army and what sorts of weapons and armor they ought to have. Jamshid invented helmets and chain mail, breastplates and swords. Jamshid did not neglect his soldiers' mounts—he even invented armor for the horses to wear. For fifty years, Jamshid worked at equipping his army, and when the fifty years were over, he had a great store of weapons and armor, greater than any other in the world.

In the next fifty years of his reign, Jamshid turned his mind to the making of thread and cloth. He invented spinning and weaving and taught the people how to take wool, flax, and silk and turn them into thread and cloth. Then, he taught the people how to cut and sew the cloth into clothing and dye the cloth to wear bright colors. The people all rejoiced in this, and so did Jamshid.

For the third fifty years, Jamshid considered how best to order the people themselves. He did this by dividing them into castes and giving each caste its place within the kingdom. The first caste was of people who spent their days in prayer and worship. Jamshid sent these to live in the mountains. The second caste was that of the warriors, the men who were skilled in battle and whose loyalty and courage supported the king's rule. The third caste was those who worked the fields and grew the crops that all might eat. These people were free and not slaves—although they had much hard labor. The fourth caste was the artisans and craftsmen, people who made good things with their hands. It took Jamshid fifty years to divide the people in this way and teach them how they must live and do their duties.

When that work was complete, Jamshid turned his mind to the creation of buildings. He told the demons under his command to take clay, use it to make bricks, and then take the bricks and use them along with stone and wood to create baths and palaces. Jamshid also opened mines so that he might have precious gems. He used magic for this and the mining of precious ores, such as silver and gold.

Jamshid discovered perfumes and taught the people how to use ambergris, sandalwood, rosewater, and many other things to create lovely scents. He also studied what things were good for medicine, and in this way, showed people how to cure illnesses and live healthy lives.

Next, Jamshid discovered how to build ships and sail them across the water. He spent another fifty years in this labor, which allowed him to travel very quickly from one place to another.

Now, Jamshid had accomplished more than any king, living or dead, but still, he was not satisfied. He built himself a golden throne, all studded with hundreds of gems.

When the throne was built, he said to the demons that served him, "Raise me up into the heavens so that my glory might shine like the sun."

Jamshid did this on the first day of the month of Farvardin, and he called that day No-Ruz, or New Day, and said that from thenceforth, it would be the first day of the year. The nobles of Jamshid's court rejoiced in this and made a great feast to celebrate, and indeed, even today, the people celebrate No-Ruz in memory of Jamshid.

For three hundred years, Jamshid's people prospered under his rule. In those days, death was unknown, the demons served the people, and the people served their king. For three hundred years, Jamshid's royal glory shone down upon his people.

Jamshid looked upon them and thought, *The whole world is mine to command. My light shines down upon the people and makes them prosperous. Who is like me? Who is more powerful than I?*

Jamshid had forgotten that he was still a man, after all, and not God.

Jamshid then summoned all his counselors and generals and wise men.

He said to them, "Who is like me? Who else rules the whole world? It was I who taught the people how to live, how to weave and sew, how to build. Every good thing that you have comes from me and my works. Surely there is no king in all the Earth but me."

The counselors, generals, and wise men all bowed their heads in assent—although they knew what Jamshid said was folly; they were too frightened of what the king might do to speak the truth to him.

But God was not afraid of Jamshid. God heard what Jamshid said and how Jamshid tried to outdo God in glory and power. On that day, God removed his glory from Jamshid. No longer did Jamshid shine upon his people as the Sun shone upon the Earth, and no longer were the people loyal to him. Some began to whisper against him, and sedition spread across the land, but it was the Arab prince Zahhak who caused Jamshid's final downfall, and now we must learn how that came about.

Zahhak the Demon Prince

In the time of Jamshid, the king of the Arabs was a kind and generous man named Merdas. He did his best to rule wisely and well. His herds numbered in the thousands, and no one who needed milk ever went without it.

Merdas had a son named Zahhak, who was as ambitious and grasping as his father was just and generous. Zahhak had an evil temper, and all who knew him understood that they had best stay out of his way. Just as Merdas had great herds of sheep and cattle that he used to feed the people, Zahhak had a great herd of horses with golden bridles for each one, and Zahhak rode everywhere to show how great and powerful he was.

One morning, a man walked up to Zahhak and said, "Greetings, O prince. I trust that you are well?"

"Yes, I am well. State your business," said Zahhak.

Now, what Zahhak did not know was that this was no ordinary man. No, it was Iblis himself, come to make a bargain.

Iblis said, "I'll tell you my business, but only if you promise not to tell anyone else what we talked about today."

"Certainly. I will keep our conversation secret."

"Good. This is why I have come to you: To give you my advice. I've seen you riding up and down on your horses with golden bridles. You're obviously a very powerful man. You could do a lot of good things if the throne were yours. Your father is old—he can't have many years left anyway, so take the throne from him. You'll be a better king than him."

"Wait, I can't do that! Yes, I do want to be king, but I'll not kill my father for it."

"You have to. If you don't do what I tell you to, you'll be breaking your promise to me. Your father will stay on the throne forever, and you'll never be anything other than a very highly placed subject."

At this, Zahhak relented. "Tell me what I have to do."

"Don't worry about it. I'll take care of everything."

Now, one of King Merdas's habits was to go into the orchard that grew near the palace each morning before sunrise. There, he would bathe and say his prayers. Both the king and the servant who accompanied him knew the way by heart, so neither had a lamp. Iblis knew this, so he went into the orchard at night and dug a deep pit along the path Merdas would be taking. When Merdas went to the orchard that morning, he fell into the pit and broke his back. Merdas died from his injuries, and as soon as Iblis saw that the king's life had departed him, he filled the pit back in with soil and left.

Zahhak soon learned of his father's misfortune. Zahhak took the throne of the Arabs and put the crown upon his head. Iblis was delighted to see that Zahhak was now on the throne.

He went to Zahhak and said, "I have some more advice for you. Do whatever I tell you, and you will have anything you could ever desire. You will be the most powerful man in the whole world."

Then, Iblis left Zahhak's court.

After a time, Iblis came back, again having disguised himself as a young man.

He went before Zahhak and said, "If it pleases your majesty, I am a very good cook and at your service."

Zahhak liked the look of the young cook, and so employed him on the spot. He gave Iblis the key to the kitchen and larders and put him in charge of preparing all the meals. In those days, people did not eat much meat, but most of the dishes that Iblis prepared for the king were made of birds' or animals' flesh. In this way, Iblis hoped to make Zahhak follow his orders, and since lions also live on the flesh of other animals, Iblis intended to make Zahhak as brave as a lion by feeding him flesh.

However, first Iblis made a dish of egg yolks for the king.

"This is a very good dish. Everyone who has ever eaten this becomes very healthy," Iblis said.

The king ate the egg yolks and found them to be delicious.

"That was a very good meal," he said and rewarded the cook.

"That was just the beginning, your majesty. Wait until you see what I will prepare tomorrow!"

The next day, Iblis prepared a dish of partridge and pheasant.

On the third day, he made a dish of chicken and lamb. Zahhak was delighted by each of these and rewarded the cook well.

On the fourth day, Iblis prepared a dish of veal cooked in wine and rosewater and seasoned with many spices. He brought it to Zahhak, and when the king had tasted it, he could not believe how good it was.

"Truly, I have never tasted anything so splendid. Whatever you want from me, you shall have it. Just name it, and it is yours," said the king.

"I am grateful to your majesty. May you live forever. Truly, your glory shall shine throughout the Earth. I have but one humble request: Allow me to kiss your shoulders."

Zahhak thought this an odd request, but he had already promised to give the cook whatever he asked, so he said, "Certainly, you may kiss my shoulders."

Iblis went up to Zahhak and kissed the king's shoulders. No sooner had Iblis finished the second kiss than he disappeared. Zahhak blinked in astonishment, but he had no time to consider that strange occurrence because something was happening to his shoulders in the places where the cook had kissed him. Zahhak looked and was appalled to see that one black snake was growing out of each shoulder. Zahhak tried everything he could think of to make the snakes go away, but nothing worked, not even cutting them off, because no matter how many times he cut them off, they would instantly grow back. Zahhak consulted every doctor he could find. He summoned doctors from faraway lands. But none of the doctors, no matter how learned, could give him a remedy.

Finally, a new doctor appeared at Zahhak's court. It was none other than Iblis, who had disguised himself yet again.

"I know these snakes distress you greatly, but I think it is your fate to bear them. The best thing you can do is feed them. They'll eat fresh meat, and that will pacify them. If you feed them human brains, though, that might kill them." Iblis said this because he was hoping that Zahhak would kill all the people to get rid of the snakes.

In this way, Iblis's desire to destroy humanity would come to pass.

The Downfall of Jamshid

Now, while Iblis was tempting Zahhak in the land of the Arabs, Jamshid was having difficulties in Persia. His royal glory no longer shone upon the land, and where he had once ruled wisely and well, he now had become ungenerous and unjust. Many of the nobles decided that they would make better kings than Jamshid, so they marshaled their own armies and staked out their own territories, saying that they had claims to the throne and would take it by force if necessary.

Some Persian nobles came to hear about the snake-shouldered king of the Arabs.

"There's a king who could help us. He'll get rid of Jamshid for sure," they said.

So, they sent an embassy to the court of Zahhak to see whether he would aid them in their quest to unseat Jamshid.

When they came before Zahhak, the ambassadors said, "O great one, surely there is no king like yourself. You rule all of Arabia, but surely your realm should be greater than that. Surely the throne of Persia also should be yours."

Zahhak listened to their flattery and decided to help them. He gathered his army and went to the aid of the Persian nobles. By this time, Jamshid had few supporters, and so his warriors could not withstand the onslaught. Jamshid was put to flight, and Zahhak put the crown of Persia upon his head.

For one hundred years, Jamshid hid from Zahhak, but Zahhak never stopped seeking him.

One day, word came to Zahhak that Jamshid had been spied near the Sea of China. Zahhak sent his soldiers to capture Jamshid. They brought Jamshid before Zahhak, and although Jamshid begged for mercy, Zahhak simply had him sawn in two.

Jamshid lived for seven hundred years, and in that time, he did many good things and many evil things. However, what good does long life do to anyone—since the world never reveals all its secrets but instead waits until we are unwary and then sends us an evil fate?

The Birth of Zal

Zal is one of the great heroes of the Shahnameh, *eclipsed only by his mighty son, Rostam. That Zal is destined for great and unusual things is signaled by the fact that he is born with white hair—a feature that seems to have been associated with demonic origins. (We will see this later in the description of the White Demon faced by Rostam.)*

Zal's father initially abandons his child, who is rescued and reared by the fearsome but kindly Simorgh, whose nurture turns the already extraordinary Zal into a great hero. The Simorgh is an animal from Persian myth with the body of a bird and the head of a lion. The Simorgh is always female, but sometimes she also has a peacock's tail. In ancient Iranian culture, the Simorgh was associated with both fertility and kingship.

Once there was a mighty warrior named Sam, who served at the court of King Manuchehr. Sam was strong, brave, and loyal, and won every battle he fought. However, he also was very sad because he had no child. He prayed many times for God to ease his sadness, and finally, those prayers were answered. One of his wives found herself with child, and when her time came, she delivered a strong, healthy boy. The baby was well made in all his limbs, and his face was the most beautiful anyone had ever seen, with lovely dark eyes. There was but one strange thing about this child: His hair was as white as snow.

The women of Sam's household were frightened to tell Sam about his child because they feared he would become angry if he knew the baby had white hair like that of an old man.

After a week had passed, the boy's wet nurse gathered all her courage and went to tell Sam about the birth of his son.

"May it please your honor, and may you live forever in great prosperity, with all your enemies under your feet, a boy child has been born to you," she said.

"Praise be to God! Finally, my desire has been fulfilled. Come, tell me about the boy. Is he healthy? Is he beautiful? How does he fare?" said Sam.

"Your son is as beautiful as a summer's day. He is well made in all his limbs. His face is as beautiful and radiant as the sun, and he has lovely dark eyes."

"Ah, that is well to hear. Tell me more."

"As I said, your honor, the boy is healthy and beautiful. There is but one thing about him that you might think ill . . . he has hair as white as snow."

Upon hearing this, Sam went immediately to the women's quarters to see his son. The boy was indeed all that the nurse had said he was: Beautiful, radiant, and strong. But all of this was marred in Sam's eyes by the boy's thatch of pure white hair.

"What have I done to deserve this? What sin have I committed that my son is cursed to look like an old man on the day of his birth? People will think that he is a demon's child, and I will never be able to show my face for shame," Sam cried.

Sam then ordered his men to take the child, now named Zal for his white hair, up into the mountains. "Expose him on the hillside. If anyone wishes to raise that wretched creature, let them take him. I want nothing more to do with him."

Thus, the child Zal was taken up into the mountains and left upon the hillside, all alone.

Now, those mountains were the home of the Simorgh, and it was there that she had her nest and raised her chicks. No sooner had Sam's men left the baby Zal on the hillside than the Simorgh flew out to find meat to feed her young. The Simorgh flew to and fro, looking for an animal or a bird that would make a good meal for her chicks. Suddenly, she heard the squall of an infant. She descended to the place the sound was coming from, and there she saw the baby, laid naked on the rock, with no one to tend him.

I wonder who left this child here, the Simorgh thought. *But no matter. Where he comes from isn't important if he'll feed my chicks.*

The Simorgh took the baby in her claws and flew back to her nest. When she arrived, she placed the baby in the nest, thinking that her chicks would feast on his flesh, but instead, something strange and wonderful happened. When the Simorgh and her young looked upon the boy and heard his cries, they pitied him and did not devour him.

The Simorgh went hunting again, this time bringing back a goat. She fed part of the goat to her young and then held up some of its flesh for the baby to suckle. In this way, the Simorgh raised Zal as though he were her own, and in time, he grew into a strong young man with mighty shoulders and a broad chest. Caravans passing near the Simorgh's dwelling sometimes caught sight of the lad, and soon tales of him began to be told throughout Persia.

Now, Sam soon heard tell of this wondrous youth with white hair, but he paid the tales no mind until one night he had a dream. In the dream, a man from India rode toward him on an Arabian horse.

The man said, "My lord, I bring you tidings of your son, Zal. He lives in the mountains, in the nest of the Simorgh. He is as strong as an ox and as brave as a lion, and his beauty is radiant like the sun."

When the man had delivered his message, Sam woke up.

Sam did not know how to understand his dream. He summoned his priests and other wise men.

He told them his dream and said, "You are the wisest men in all Persia. What do you think this means?"

The priests and wise men replied, "All creatures of the world love their young and rear them with kindness. Even the most vicious leopard takes care of her cubs. But you have treated your son most evilly. You cast him out when he was but an infant, leaving him to die on the mountainside. You should pray to God for forgiveness, for your sin has been great."

Sam's heart was troubled by these words, and when night fell, he had another dream. He dreamed he was in India, at the foot of a mountain. Before him was a great army, led by a beautiful slave. On one side of the slave was a wise sage, and on the other, a priest.

One of these came forward and said to Sam, "You have greatly sinned before God. You prayed for a son, yet when God granted your wish, you cast your son out into the wilderness. Why should white hair trouble you so? After all, your hair and beard are white as snow, yet you count yourself a good man. It is fortunate that God's love is greater than your shame and that he sent the Simorgh to look after your child—the child you asked for and then despised."

At this, Sam cried out in his sleep.

In the morning, Sam summoned his chief advisers and the leaders of his army and set out for the mountains where the Simorgh lived. Sam traveled through the mountains until he finally came to the highest and sheerest of all the peaks, and on the very top was the nest of the Simorgh. The nest was made from ebony and sandalwood woven together and looked like a great palace.

When Sam saw the Simorgh's nest, he fell to his knees and bowed his face to the ground.

Not lifting his eyes, he prayed, "O God who made all things, I give thanks to you for the great Simorgh, the mightiest of all your creatures. You who are the most just and the most powerful, hear my prayer. If the youth who lives with the Simorgh is indeed my son and not the child of a demon, help me find my way to him."

As Sam was kneeling and making his prayer, the Simorgh spied him there at the foot of the mountain, and she knew the time had come for her human son to return to his people.

The Simorgh said to the young man, "You have grown up in my nest and are like one of my own chicks. But now your human father waits at the foot of the mountain, and I must return you to him."

"I do not want to leave. This is my home. Have I been a burden? Is that why you wish to dispose of me?" said Zal.

The Simorgh replied, "This nest may have been your home, but fate has an even more glorious home in store for you. Your father is none other than the hero Sam, who lives in a palace far more beautiful than my nest. Here, take two of my feathers. If ever you need me, place a feather in the fire and summon me. I will take the form of a black cloud and come to fetch you back here."

Then the Simorgh gently took the youth in her claws and flew down to where his father was waiting. Her heart was very heavy, for she did not want to part with the young man whom she had raised as her own. The Simorgh set Zal down gently in front of Sam, who bowed low before the great bird and did her much honor.

When Sam looked at his son, he wept tears of joy, for Zal was even more beautiful than the tales had said. He was tall and strong, with a mighty chest and mighty limbs, and his white hair flowed over his shoulders down to the middle of his body. Sam threw a cloak over his son's body and led him down the mountainside, where the youth was dressed in clothing befitting a king. Then Sam mounted Zal on the finest of his horses.

When the army saw Sam's son, they cheered and rejoiced, for none of them had ever seen a youth as beautiful or as strong, and they were glad that he was reunited with his father. Sam ordered that drummers be mounted on elephants and lead the army, playing all the way home.

At the gates of the city, all manner of musicians awaited Sam's return. As soon as they saw his army approaching, they let up a great din of trumpets, cymbals, and drums to celebrate Sam's homecoming with his son Zal, and all the city set to feasting in celebration.

The Seven Trials of Rostam

Rostam is perhaps the greatest hero in ancient Persian myth. The son of Zal, whom we met in the previous story, has all the qualities one would expect of such a champion. Rostam is supernaturally strong and skilled with weaponry, and he is so tall and heavy, even as a very young man, that no ordinary horse can bear his weight. A significant number of the tales in the Shahnameh *are dedicated to the exploits of Rostam.*

Rostam's closest companion is Rakhsh, a stallion who can understand human speech. Like Rostam, Rakhsh has supernatural qualities. He is a chestnut roan, but instead of the usual white hairs mixed in with the chestnut, Rakhsh has golden hairs. Of all the horses in Persia, only Rakhsh is big and strong enough to carry both Rostam and his weapons, one of which is a giant mace.

"The Seven Trials of Rostam" relates the deeds of Rostam as he rides out to rescue the Persian King Kavus and his army after they have fallen into the clutches of an evil demon during a campaign to destroy Mazandaran, a country under the sway of evil beings. It is Rostam's father, Zal, who orders him to effect this rescue, telling him that this deed is the reason why Rostam was born and what he was

meant to do. Rostam readily agrees and promises not to return unless he is victorious.

(Note on terminology: In this story, distances are given in ancient Persian units called parasangs*. One parasang was the distance a man could walk in an hour, and is equivalent to about six kilometers or about three miles.)*

The First Trial: The Lion

When Rostam heard that King Kavus and his army were in the clutches of an evil demon, he took up his weapons, saddled his horse, and set out on the road that would bring him to Mazandaran. Rostam rode all day and into the night, and when dawn came, he found himself to be tired and hungry.

He rode on until he came to a plain where a herd of wild asses was grazing. Rostam took out his lariat and urged Rakhsh into a gallop. Rostam and Rakhsh chased down one of the asses, and soon Rostam had captured one and killed it. Rostam then built a fire and skinned the ass, and when all was ready, he roasted the meat and ate it straight off the bone. However, Rostam did not only think about his hunger; he removed Rakhsh's bridle and turned him loose to graze on the good grass that grew in that place.

His hunger sated, Rostam went to the nearby river, where he cut enough reeds to make himself a comfortable bed. He lay down by the fire and fell asleep, while Rakhsh stood guard over him.

Now, Rostam and Rakhsh were unaware that behind the reed bed was the den of a lion. The lion had been out hunting when Rostam arrived, but he came home soon after Rostam went to sleep. The lion looked at the giant of a warrior who lay on a bed of reeds, and then he looked at the warrior's horse. Calculating that it would be wise to kill the horse first, the lion pounced at Rakhsh. The lion was no match for the horse. Rakhsh met the lion's assault with his hooves, splitting the lion's skull asunder. Then Rakhsh sank his teeth into the lion's back and tossed the animal onto the ground, where Rakhsh proceeded to trample it with his hooves until the lion was quite dismembered.

Rostam awoke during the night and saw what remained of the lion.

He said to Rakhsh, "Why did you deal with that lion all by yourself? That wasn't a very smart thing to do, not when I was here to help you. What would I have done if the lion had killed you? I can't very well walk all the way to Mazandaran. Next time, wake me up. Don't fight by yourself."

The Second Trial: The Spring of Water

In the morning, Rostam said his prayers, and then gave Rakhsh a rubdown and put on his saddle. Rostam took up his weapons and mounted the horse. He urged Rakhsh forward, and so they began the next portion of their journey.

Their way forward led across a desert, and after many miles, both Rostam and Rakhsh were beset by thirst. Rakhsh was stumbling with weariness and panting, while Rostam was weak in his body, and his lips were parched and cracked. Rostam dismounted and led Rakhsh by the reins.

Rostam turned his eyes to Heaven and said, "Almighty God, I pray you for mercy. You know that my task is to rescue King Kavus from the demons and that I do this because you command it. Have mercy upon us all, we who walk this earth and are tormented by thirst."

No sooner had he finished his prayer than the mighty Rostam fell to the dusty earth, unable to take even one more step forward. Just then, a fat ram ran across the path, and Rostam's spirits rose.

"Come, Rakhsh. Let's follow that ram. It's so sleek and fat—there must be water nearby. God surely has sent the ram as a sign of his mercy and compassion," he said.

Rostam and Rakhsh followed the ram, which soon led them to a freshwater stream that flowed along merrily.

Rostam said, "Surely the one true God is the only God, and blessed are those who trust in him!" Then he cried after the ram, "Blessings upon you, friend! May you always have the best of grass and the clearest of water, and may no beast take you as its prey! May no hunter's arrows ever strike you! If not for you, my horse and I would surely be carrion for the vultures!"

Rostam unsaddled Rakhsh, and both of them drank deeply. Rostam took off all his clothing and bathed in the clear, cool water, and when he was thus refreshed, he found that he was hungry. Therefore, he took his bow and arrows and went in search of something to eat. He came upon a wild ass, which he brought down with an arrow and then skinned. He roasted the meat over an open fire and ate the meat straight off the bone. When his meal was done, he went back to the stream and drank deeply of the fresh water.

Satisfied body and soul, Rostam lay down near the fire and said to Rakhsh, "Remember what I said: No fighting by yourself. Wake me if any demons or dangerous beasts come here."

Then Rostam went to sleep, and Rakhsh grazed nearby, keeping watch over his friend.

The Third Trial: The Dragon

Rakhsh grazed peacefully until midnight when, in the distance, he spied a huge dragon heading toward him and Rostam. He nudged Rostam awake, but when Rostam arose, the dragon hid in the shadows so that Rostam saw nothing.

"Jumping at shadows, old friend?" said Rostam, who was annoyed at having been awoken. "Don't wake me up unless there's something really there."

Then Rostam lay down and went back to sleep.

As soon as the dragon saw that Rostam had returned to his rest, he again started slithering toward the hero's camp. Again, Rakhsh woke Rostam, and again, the dragon hid so that Rostam saw nothing. Rostam was very angry this time.

"What is wrong with you? I swear, if you wake me up again and I see there's nothing there, I'll cut off your feet and walk all the way to Mazandaran," said Rostam.

He lay down a third time and went back to sleep, and a third time, the dragon resumed its path toward the hero. Smoke and flames billowed from its mouth, but Rakhsh dared not wake Rostam a third time. Rakhsh bolted away from the monster, but then his love for Rostam brought him galloping back. This time, instead of waking Rostam gently, Rakhsh neighed and stamped at the ground. Rostam awoke, utterly furious, but this time, the dragon did not hide quickly enough, and Rostam saw it.

Rostam drew his sword and said to the dragon, "Tell me your name. I don't like killing my enemies without knowing who they are, and I intend to kill you."

The dragon replied, "I am he who rules in this place. My claws are sharper than spear points, and neither man nor beast dares tread upon this land. Even eagles fear to fly above it, and the stars fear to shine. Now tell me your name because your mother will soon weep for you."

"I am Rostam, son of Zal, son of Sam, of the line of Nariman," said Rostam, and at that, the dragon leaped at him, and a battle ensued.

Rostam fought well, but soon the dragon used its weight against him, and Rostam faltered. When Rakhsh saw this, he raced in to help his friend, barreling into the dragon with his own body and knocking the great, snaky beast back. Then Rakhsh attacked with hooves and teeth, and even Rostam wondered at the horse's ferocity.

Finally, Rostam saw his chance. He slashed with his sword, cutting the monster's head clean off its body. Poisonous blood gushed out of the wound, seeping into the desert floor and dissolving the very soil. Rostam had never seen so much blood and had never known a poison so deadly, and he was afraid. He went into a nearby stream and bathed his body and clothing, praying all the while.

When his prayer and bath alike were done, Rostam mounted his horse and resumed his journey.

The Fourth Trial: The Witch

Rostam rode through what was left of the night and into the next day. When the sun had begun to set, he arrived at a fair country shaded by many trees, through which a river of clear water was running. Near the river, a meal had been set out, with roasted fowl heaped high on platters, and bowls mounded full of rice mixed with dates and spices, and fresh cucumbers and candied fruits, and goblets of wine, and fine cushions for the guests to sit on. This was a feast set out for the sorcerers who lived in that land, but the sorcerers had run away and hid when they heard Rakhsh's hoofbeats approaching.

Rostam dismounted and unsaddled Rakhsh when he saw the feast spread before him, with no one there to enjoy it. He then sat down in front of the food and noticed a lute among the cushions, platters, and plates. Rostam picked up the lute and began to play it. To amuse himself, he made up a song to go along with the melody he played.

Rostam am I, hero brave and bold,
My days are numbered, I won't live to be old.
A paladin, I travel to where the battles are,
I have no feather bed, I sleep under the stars.
Demons, dragons, warriors all
Beneath the might of my sword do fall.
Across deserts bright and mountains high
I journey on and on, and rarely do I
Find a resting place of peace and plenty,
With wine and song and friends about me.
No, to fight with demons is my fate,

For that's the hero's true estate.

Now, among the sorcerers was a witch, and when she heard Rostam's song, she decided to see what manner of man he was. She disguised herself as a beautiful young woman dressed in the finest of silks, with flowing black hair and lovely dark eyes.

She sat down next to Rostam and said, "Greetings, stranger. Please, partake of the food and wine, but as you do so, tell me who you are and where you are from."

When the woman sat down, Rostam could scarcely believe his luck, and he praised God in his heart for sending him not only such good food and drink but also a beautiful woman to share it with.

Rostam handed the woman a goblet of wine and said, "I am Rostam and have traveled very far. Give thanks to God with me that this feast is here and that we may enjoy it together."

At the mention of God's name, the witch's face blurred and twisted.

Rostam quickly took his lariat and ensnared the witch's head with it, and when he had her well tied up, Rostam said, "Tell me who you really are. Show me your true self."

The young woman's face and body changed until a withered old hag stood before Rostam. She cursed both God and Rostam, and at this, Rostam knew her to be a witch.

He took his dagger and cut her in two, and when the other sorcerers saw this, they were frightened and remained in hiding.

The Fifth Trial: The Capture of Olad

Rostam left the sorcerers' land behind him and rode until he came to a country where all was black as night. Neither the Sun nor Moon nor stars were visible. Rostam picked his way forward as carefully as he could, not knowing what the road underfoot would prove to be like, nor what might be coming toward him and his valiant horse in the pitch blackness. For all its horrors, the dark country proved to be a relatively small place, and soon Rostam and Rakhsh emerged into the light as from behind a curtain, and they found themselves in a peaceful place full of green, rolling hills and pleasant fields in which the young wheat was growing. The Sun was shining, and the air was very warm, and soon Rostam found that his clothing and helmet were soaked with sweat. Feeling the need for some rest, Rostam dismounted and took off Rakhsh's bridle so that he could graze. Then Rostam took off his helmet and his armor, which was made of a tiger's skin, and when his helmet and clothing had dried, he put the helmet and his armor back on and then lay down to sleep while Rakhsh nibbled on the shoots of fresh wheat.

Rostam had not been sleeping long when a man who had been set to guard the wheat saw Rakhsh wandering through the field and eating his fill. The man ran over to where Rostam lay and poked at his legs with a stick.

"You! Hey, you there! Wake up! Is that your horse? Why did you turn him loose there? Don't you know this is someone else's land? What makes you think it's all right to let your horse ruin a perfectly good crop? Get your horse and leave! You're not welcome here."

Rostam woke up, enraged at the man's words and at being unceremoniously poked with a stick. Rostam jumped up, grabbed hold of the man's ears, and then twisted them right off his head and threw them to the ground.

"You . . . you demon!" screamed the man. "You devil! You Ahriman in the flesh! How dare you! Wait until my master hears about this!"

Then the man picked up his ears and ran away.

Now, the servant who had been watching the wheat worked for a man name Olad. Olad was a fine young man of good family and had spent the day hunting with his friends. The servant ran up to Olad just as he was arriving home and inviting his friends inside for some wine. The servant showed his bloody ears to Olad and told him about the horrible man and monstrous horse ruining the wheat fields. Olad quickly remounted his horse, as did his friends, and they all rode off like the wind to see whom it was trampling Olad's crops.

When Rostam saw Olad and his friends riding toward him, he mounted Rakhsh and drew his glittering sword.

Olad reined in his steed before Rostam and said, "Tell me your name and who you serve. This is my land, and we don't let violent men do whatever they please here."

"My name is Rostam, and that name should freeze your blood. Surely, you've heard of me? You should know that no matter how many men you bring against me, you will never defeat me."

Then Rostam charged toward the group of young noblemen and began laying about him with his sword. Olad and his friends wheeled their horses around and fled, but not before several of the young men had been beheaded by Rostam.

Rostam gave chase on Rakhsh. As soon as he was within range, he took his lariat and lassoed Olad with it, pulling him off his horse. Rostam then jumped down and tied him up.

"Now, if you know what's good for you, you'll tell me what I want to know, and you'll tell me the truth. Tell me where I can find the White Demon and the demons Kulad Ghandi and Bid, and tell me where King Kavus and his army are being held prisoner. Do right by me, and I'll see that you're made king of Mazandaran when I'm done dealing with my enemies in that country."

Olad replied, "There's no need for violence. I'll tell you everything you want to know, and I'll tell you the truth. I'll show you where the White Demon is and how to get to where Kavus is. The demons dwell about one hundred parasangs from here. The place where Kavus resides is one hundred parasangs further on, and the entire two hundred parasangs is a journey full of peril. The whole place is crawling with demons led by Kulad Ghandi, with Bid and Sanjeh fighting at his side, and although you may think yourself quite fierce and warlike, you have nothing on the creatures that live in those places.

"Next, you'll have to pass through a land called Bargush, where all the people have dogs' heads, and if you thought Kulad Ghandi and his crew were bad, just wait until you see what awaits you on the other side of Bargush. There are six hundred thousand well-mounted soldiers there, all with the finest weapons and armor, and on top of that, there are twelve hundred war elephants. No one can survive running that gauntlet, not even the great Rostam."

When Rostam heard this, he laughed aloud. "That journey doesn't sound at all difficult. Anyway, when those demons see me coming, they'll all run away screaming, but it will be to no avail because I'll hunt down every last one of them and cleave them in two with my sword. And the ones I don't cleave, I'll crush with my mace. It's going to be a big job, so we'd better get started. Lead the way!"

The Sixth Trial: The Battle with Arzhang

Rostam and Olad rode onward all through the rest of the day and into the following night. When they arrived at the plain at the foot of Mount Aspruz, where the demons had defeated Kavus and his army, they could see the campfires of a great army in the distance ahead of them.

Suddenly, a great shouting and roaring went up into the night, and Rostam said to Olad, "What is this place? Who is making that terrible racket?"

"That is the camp of the demons who guard the border of Mazandaran. Kulad Ghandi is their leader, and the demons Arzhang and Bid are there too. The whole army has pledged their loyalty to the White Demon, and they're the ones making the noise," replied Olad.

"Right, we'll stop here for the night. This seems as safe a place as any. We'll get some sleep, but don't even think of running away if you value your life."

Rostam and Olad slept, and in the morning, Rostam tied Olad to a tree and took up his weapons. He mounted Rakhsh and set off toward Mazandaran, his helmet on his head and his tiger-skin armor on his body. On the way, he thought about how he might go about defeating his enemy and decided to look first for Arzhang and then see what he should do from there. When Rostam arrived at the edge of the demons' camp, he gave a great war cry. It was so loud that it echoed off all the mountains and split boulders in half.

Arzhang heard Rostam's cry and came rushing out of his tent to see who had made such a fearsome sound. Rostam saw Arzhang come out of his tent, so he urged Rakhsh into a gallop. Rostam roared into the demons' camp, and when he got close to Arzhang, he picked the demon up by the ears and ripped his head off with his bare hands. He then threw Arzhang's head to one side and his body to the other and drew his mace. The demons who had rushed to Arzhang's defense saw Rostam start to swing his mace and fled in terror. Rostam drew his sword and rode after them, laying about him first on one side and then on the other, until all the demons had either been slain or run into the mountains to hide.

The battle done, Rostam rode back to where he had made camp the night before and released Olad from the tree.

"Right, that's Arzhang and his crew dealt with. Now lead me to King Kavus," said Rostam.

Olad led Rostam to the city where the demons had housed the king and his army. As soon as they arrived on the outskirts, Rakhsh gave a great neigh that rang through the air.

Inside the city, Kavus said, "Did you hear that? That was Rakhsh neighing! Rostam is here, and soon we will be free!"

No sooner had Kavus said these words than Rostam rode up to him. The Persians all crowded around, cheering, and Kavus greeted Rostam with great joy.

"Oh, most welcome to you, Rostam! Never have you been so welcome to me. Come, tell us about your journey, and tell us how your father Zal is doing."

"My father is doing very well, O my king, except that he is greatly troubled by your plight and waits every day for word that you will be returning home. My journey has been long, but I have already killed Arzhang and many of his followers, and I hope to rid the earth of the rest of them before this is over," replied Rostam.

"I also await the day that I will return home, with much impatience, but that day will not come if you do not hurry and kill the White Demon as soon as you can. Once he hears of Arzhang's death, he will send swarms of his demon-soldiers out of the mountains, and there will be so many of them that even you, Rostam, will not be able to withstand them. To get to the White Demon's lair, you'll have to go into the mountains, which are all patrolled by demon soldiers. In the mountains, you'll find a great cavern that seems like nothing other than a black maw waiting to swallow you whole. That is where the White Demon lives. If you go into the cavern and kill him, the other demons will run away because they won't know what to do once they are leaderless.

"But listen, Rostam. We're more than just prisoners here—the demons have taken our eyesight. That's why they can put us in this city and not worry about guards. If you can, bring us back some of the White Demon's blood. Learned doctors have told us that this is the cure for our blindness if we use it as a balm on our eyes."

"I will leave right away, then. I'm going to track down this White Demon and destroy him, and hopefully, God will give me the strength I need. Otherwise, you'll have to languish here for who knows how long. But keep up your courage! I've never been defeated yet, and I'm sure that soon you'll be back home with your families."

The Seventh Trial: The Battle with the White Demon

Rostam readied himself for his battle with the White Demon and then rode toward the mountains with Olad as his guide. Soon enough, they could see the cavern Kavus had described and the many demon soldiers that stood between Rostam and the White Demon's lair.

Rostam said to Olad, "You have been faithful to your promise to tell me the truth. Now I ask you for the truth one more time. Tell me how I can get through those soldiers so that I can find the White Demon and kill him."

Olad replied, "You need to wait until noon when the Sun is highest and the day is warmest. The light and the heat make the demons go to sleep, and they'll be easy to conquer then. Be warned: A few of them are sorcerers, and they don't ever sleep at all. But if God is on your side, you should be able to defeat them easily."

Rostam took Olad's advice and waited until noon to ride to the White Demon's cave. When midday arrived, he tied Olad up with his lariat. Then he mounted Rakhsh, roared out his name so that all the mountains echoed with the sound, drew his sword, and rode forward to engage his foes. The demons never stood a chance, for Rostam rode through their ranks like a scythe through hay. He slashed off the heads of every single demon, and soon all of them lay dead.

Next, Rostam readied himself to enter the White Demon's cave. Never had Rostam seen a cave so dark and dank, and never had he faced such a fearsome enemy. He stood in front of the entrance to the cave for a moment, his heart racing with hope and fear. Then he stepped forward and peered into the shadows, trying to see his enemy. At first, he could see nothing but blackness, but after a time, a huge shape became visible within the darkness. Rostam continued staring at the shape, and soon he could make out a huge head of white hair atop a black body that was the size of a small mountain. Suddenly, the shape leaped at Rostam, and Rostam saw what it was: It was the White Demon, clad in armor like himself, ready and willing to do battle.

Rostam nearly quailed, for he had never seen any foe as large or strong or deadly. However, he summoned all his courage and slashed at the White Demon. His sword found its mark, lopping off one of the demon's legs at mid-thigh. This didn't stop the demon, though; wounded as he was, he propelled himself at Rostam, and soon the two of them were locked in close combat, rolling on the ground and punching and gouging at each other until the dust was so mixed with their blood that it turned into red mud. So strong and skilled was the demon that Rostam began to despair of his life.

But I can't stop now. Either I die here, or I kill this demon. Because if I run away, I have no hope of conquering Mazandaran. They'll all just laugh at me, he thought.

This thought gave Rostam new courage. He roared out his battle cry and threw the demon to the ground. Then, Rostam drew his dagger and slit the demon's throat, killing him. Rostam then cut the demon's heart and liver out of his body. When the whirl of combat was done, Rostam looked about him and saw, as if for the first time, how very large the White Demon was, and how very much blood he and his enemy had spilled.

Rostam rode back to the place where he had left Olad and released him from his bonds.

He handed the demon's liver to Olad, who said, "Never have I seen such a warrior as yourself. Even a lion would not have escaped from that combat alive. I now have hope that you will keep your word to me, and make me King of Mazandaran, for surely it would not be worthy of such a victor as yourself to go back on that promise."

Rostam replied, "I shall certainly keep my word to you and make you the king of this land. But before that can happen, we have many tasks to do and many battles to fight. There is the King of Mazandaran to deal with and hordes upon hordes of demons. But we will conquer, and then you will rule."

Rostam Returns to Kavus

Rostam and Olad rode back to the city where Kavus and his men were waiting.

Rostam went before the king and said, "O my king, hear now of my victory over the White Demon. I went into his cave and did dire battle with him, but in the end, I slit his throat and cut out his liver. What deed might I do next for your glorious majesty?"

"May you be forever and ever blessed, and may my kingdom never be without your aid and the might of your arm. And may your mother and father be forever blessed for giving my kingdom such a champion," replied Kavus.

Then, Rostam took some blood from the demon's liver and smeared it on Kavus's eyes, and the king's sight was restored. Rostam restored the sight of all of Kavus's soldiers, who then set up an ivory throne for their king.

Kavus sat upon the throne and held a council of war with Rostam and the army's generals, each one of them a mighty hero in his own right. When their plans were laid, the men held a great feast to celebrate their freedom and the defeat of the White Demon.

After a week of music, dancing, and wine, Kavus and his men put on their armor and took up their weapons. They went through the cities of Mazandaran as a raging fire goes through a field of dry grass.

Neither man nor woman nor child withstood the wrath of Kavus and his generals, but soon Kavus called a halt to the slaughter, saying, "We have meted out the punishment that this land deserves, so we will stop our pillaging for now. It is time to send a message to the King of Mazandaran, to give him a choice about whether he lives or dies, and about what befalls his country."

The First Letter to the King of Mazandaran

King Kavus summoned his scribe and told him to take down a letter on the finest white silk and perfume it with musk. This is what the letter said:

> *From Kavus, King of Persia, to the King of Mazandaran, greetings. We give thanks to God for having made the heavens and the earth and giving us the ability to choose between good and evil. If you follow the true faith and deal justly with your fellows, then everyone will call you blessed, but if you turn away from God and do evil, then evil surely shall befall you. Have you not seen what has befallen your soldiers? Have you not seen the fates of Arzhang, of Kulad Ghandi, of Bid, of the White Demon? You should know that the only way to save yourself is to give way to me and become one of my subjects because if you continue to resist, I shall have no choice but to loose the hero Rostam onto your kingdom, and there is no escape from the might of his arm. Bow to me, and pay Persia tribute, and you will live and continue to rule as King of Mazandaran. Defy me, and your fate will be the same as that of Arzhang, the White Demon, and every other demon that has been slain these past few days.*

When the letter was written and sealed, King Kavus gave it to one of his generals, a man named Farhad, who was known not only for his skill with a sword but also for his great probity.

"Take this letter to the King of Mazandaran, and we shall see whether he has any wisdom in that demonic head of his," said Kavus.

Farhad bowed to the king and then rode off to the land of the Gorgsaran, a place where the people's feet were made of leather, and the warriors fought with long, sharp daggers. This land was the place where the King of Mazandaran was residing at the time.

When the king heard that a messenger from Kavus was on his way there, the king sent three of his best warriors out to greet him.

"Go and meet this fellow, and mind you give him as much grief as you can. Provoke him into fighting with you. Do whatever it takes," said the king.

The warriors went to Farhad, looking as fierce and warlike as they possibly could. They tried harassing him with words, but Farhad remained cool and calm. When one of the warriors shook hands with Farhad, he squeezed so hard that many of Farhad's bones were broken, but Farhad made no sign that he felt any pain. The warriors gave up trying to provoke Farhad and brought him before their king.

"Welcome. I hope your ruler is doing well and that your journey was not too unpleasant," said the king.

"My king is well, thank you, and the journey was not arduous," said Farhad.

"Tell me your errand."

"I bring you a letter from King Kavus." Farhad handed the letter to the King of Mazandaran.

The king gave the letter to one of his scribes and said, "Read this aloud."

The scribe began to read, and when the king heard of the fates of Arzhang and the White Demon, his heart filled up with grief. When the king heard about the might of Rostam and his deeds, his grief mixed with rage. By the time the scribe finished reading, the king's eyes were filled with tears.

"Take silk and pen," the king said to the scribe, "and write down this reply to Kavus, the king of the Persians. 'To Kavus, King of Persia, from the King of Mazandaran, greetings. I have heard your letter and think you foolish to assume that your kingdom is more glorious than mine. I have an army of my own, and its might will overwhelm you. Every one of your warriors will be deprived of his head, and you will be utterly defeated.'"

When Farhad heard what the King of Mazandaran said, he did not wait to be given the letter. Instead, he mounted his horse and raced back to King Kavus.

Farhad told the king everything that had befallen him on his mission and related to him the reply that the king of Mazandaran intended to send. Rostam was there and heard everything Farhad said.

Rostam said to Kavus, "Send me to the king next. Write another letter, one that leaves no doubt about your warlike intent or the might of your army. I'll bring the letter and make some threats of my own."

Kavus agreed to this plan, saying, "Yes, let us do as you say. Even the King of Mazandaran will quail before you—neither man nor beast nor demon has yet been created who can withstand your strength and skill."

The Second Letter to the King of Mazandaran

When the scribe was ready with silk and ink, Kavus dictated this letter to the King of Mazandaran:

> *From Kavus, King of Persia, to the King of Mazandaran, greetings. I have read your letter and wonder how a man who should be wise stoops to saying such foolish things. Bow down to me as my subject. You have no other choice if you want to keep your life and your kingdom. Continue to defy me, and your kingdom will be mine anyway, and your rotting corpse will be left on the battlefield as food for the vultures.*

The scribe wrote the letter, sealed it, and then gave it to Kavus. Kavus gave it to Rostam, who mounted Rakhsh and galloped away on his mission. The King of Mazandaran's guards saw Rostam approaching from afar.

One of them ran to tell the king the news. "O my king, another messenger from Kavus is on his way, but I've never seen his like. His shoulders are as broad as those of two men, and surely, he has the strength of a lion or maybe even an elephant. He has a fine lariat hanging from his saddle and a mace that even our mightiest warrior would struggle to lift. He is galloping here on a horse that is just as fearsome as he is."

The King of Mazandaran chose three of his best warriors and said, "Go out and greet this new messenger. You know what to do."

When Rostam saw the warriors coming to greet him, he dismounted Rakhsh near a large tree. Rostam pulled up the tree by its roots and waved it around as though it were a lance. Then Rostam threw the tree down and rode to meet the warriors, who had stopped in their tracks and gaped in astonishment at what Rostam was doing.

"Greetings! I come from King Kavus and have a message for the King of Mazandaran," said Rostam.

"Greetings to you. We have come to bring you to our ruler," said the chief warrior.

The warrior held out his hand for a handshake and attempted to crush Rostam's hand but found his own crushed instead by a smiling Rostam. So great was the pain that the warrior fainted and fell off his horse. The fall brought him back to consciousness, so he remounted and rode back with his companions to tell their king what had happened.

The king summoned a warrior named Kolahvar. Kolahvar was an expert horseman and the most skilled fighter in the whole kingdom. Everyone feared him because he was fierce as a leopard and liked nothing better than going to war and slaying his enemies.

The king said to Kolahvar, "Go out and meet this messenger. Show him what you're made of. Shame him so badly that he cries."

Kolahvar rode out to meet Rostam. He made himself look as fierce as possible and shouted many belligerent questions at the Persian hero. When Kolahvar finally decided to shake hands with Rostam, he squeezed so hard that Rostam's hand was badly bruised, but Rostam gave no sign that he felt any discomfort. In return, Rostam squeezed Kolahvar's hand so tightly that all his fingernails popped off. Kolahvar rode back to the king and showed him his useless hand.

"Look at what he did to me! If you have any wisdom at all, you'll give in and make yourself subject to the King of Persia. It's the best way to protect your people and yourself because there's no way we'll be able to stand against this warrior and Kavus's army," said Kolahvar.

Just as Kolahvar finished speaking, Rostam strode into the throne room and stood before the king.

The king asked him to be seated and then said, "So, you have come from Kavus? How is he faring? How fares his army?"

"Yes, my Lord. I am a messenger from King Kavus, who fares well, as does his army," replied Rostam.

"I heard about what you did to Kolahvarl. Surely you must be Rostam? No one else has that kind of strength."

"Oh, no, I'm not Rostam. I'm not even worthy of being his servant. He's much stronger and much more skilled than I am." Then Rostam gave Kavus's letter to the King of Mazandaran, saying, "Here is my ruler's reply to your foolish letter. You really should do the wise thing and capitulate. My sword rests uneasily in its sheath and longs to make its way through the necks of your warriors."

The King of Mazandaran was enraged by Kavus's letter and Rostam's bold words. "You go back to that so-called king of yours and tell him this: I will never bow to him as a subject, and I will pay him no tribute. Tell him that his overweening pride will be his downfall because he has goaded me beyond endurance. I will muster my army and attack him, and when I meet him face to face in battle, only one of us will be left standing, and that one will be me."

Rostam looked at the King of Mazandaran and his generals with disdain.

"Very well. You have sealed your doom," he said.

Then, he strode out of the hall and rode back to tell Kavus everything he had seen and heard.

"Don't worry about that fool and his army. They're no match for us. Let's get ready and make our battle plan. We have hordes of demons to destroy!" said Rostam.

The Battle Between the King of Mazandaran and the King of Persia

As soon as Rostam departed to return to Kavus, the King of Mazandaran began to muster his army and confer with his generals about their plan of attack. He had the royal pavilion packed to bring to the battlefield, and when his army was assembled and on the march, they put up so much dust as they went along that the mountains behind them were obscured, and the sky was darkened. That army was mighty and fearsome as besides warriors who went on foot and horseback, hundreds of war elephants were trained to fight just as fiercely as any human warrior.

A messenger told Kavus that the King of Mazandaran was approaching with his army, so Kavus summoned Rostam and his generals to make their plan of attack. When everyone agreed as to what was to be done, the army was assembled and the generals placed in command. They pitched their pavilions on the plain and arrayed their warriors according to their plan. Trumpeters blew their war fanfares, and the mountains rang with the sound. Kavus had such a large army that it seemed to be a forest of trees made of steel. King Kavus marched in the center of his army, while Rostam rode at the head.

When both armies had arrived at the plain, they halted, waiting for the battle to begin. But first, a great warrior from Mazandaran rode up to the Persian army. The warrior's name was Juyan, and he was the best fighter with a mace in his entire country.

Juyan rode back and forth in front of the Persians and shouted, "A challenge! Who will fight with me, champion to champion? Who will prove which is the mightier?"

The Persians heard Juyan's voice and saw how imposing he was, so none of them dared answer his challenge.

Kavus said, "Do you have blood in your veins or water? Are none of you true Persian men? Who will fight with this Juyan?"

When none of the Persian warriors replied, Rostam went to the king and said, "I'll fight him, your majesty. Let me do this deed."

Kavus replied, "The deed is yours. Go in victory."

Rostam took his lance and galloped onto the plain between the armies. He sent up a war cry that echoed off the mountains and made the whole battlefield shake.

Then, he called out to Juyan, "Who do you think you are, to challenge the army of the King of Persia? Go home, or else your mother will mourn you. Leave the service of the demon you call king—you are not worthy of the name of warrior otherwise."

Juyan said, "Bold words, but words don't frighten me. You should go home yourself. My dagger will turn your armor into shreds, and it is your mother who will be weeping."

When Rostam heard Juyan's words, he urged Rakhsh into a gallop. Rostam flung his lance as hard as he could at Juyan, and it hit him in the middle of his body. So hard did Rostam throw the lance that it went through Juyan's armor as though it were made of silk and was stuck there in the middle of his body, the head of the lance poking out through the warrior's back. Rostam rode up to Juyan and flung him to the ground, the lance still transfixing his body. The Mazandaran soldiers paled when they saw what Rostam did to Juyan.

The King of Mazandaran saw what was happening to his soldiers, so he shouted, "Men of Mazandaran! Have courage! We are the greater army, and our resolve is the strongest! Attack now! Victory to Mazandaran!"

War drums pounded and war trumpets blared on both sides as the armies advanced upon one another, and soon battle was joined. Swords flashed, steel clashed on steel, elephants brayed, and horses neighed as the two armies battered one another. Back and forth the battle went for a week, with neither army able to claim the victory.

When the eighth day dawned with no end to the war in sight, an exhausted Kavus took off his helmet and knelt on the battlefield.

"Lord God of the heavens, hear my prayer. If ever I have found favor in your eyes, grant me the victory over these demons," he said.

Then, Kavus put his helmet back on and mustered his army for yet another attack. Again and again, the Persians battered the Mazandaran forces. The Persian generals fought like lions, and Rostam seemed to be everywhere at once, demons falling at his feet like leaves from a tree in autumn.

Rostam and his companions fought their way toward the place where the King of Mazandaran was making his stand, but they could not break through the Mazandaran ranks. Rostam handed his lance to his squire and took up his mace instead. Wherever he struck with his mace, he dealt a death blow, whether to soldier or horse or elephant, and soon the ground around him was piled with corpses, and the Mazandaran army in rout—although the king and his companions still fought fiercely.

Rostam looked up and saw that he had a chance to kill the king. He took back his lance and hurled it with all his might. The lance went right through the king's armor and lodged itself in his spine, but instead of falling off his horse, dead, the king turned himself into a giant granite boulder, nearly as big as a small hill. Even Rostam was stopped in his tracks by this astonishing thing. Kavus saw Rostam standing there, agape, and rode up to him.

"Why are you standing there staring?" asked Kavus.

"I was in the midst of battle and working my way toward the King of Mazandaran. I laid about me with my mace and set the Mazandaran army into rout. Then, I took my lance and hurled it at the king. The lance transfixed his body, but instead of falling off his horse, he turned himself into this huge rock that you see before you."

Kavus ordered that the rock be taken back to the Persian camp. The strongest Persian men gathered around the rock and tried to pick it up, but they could not move it. Then, Rostam walked up to the rock, wrapped his arms around it, and with one great heave lifted it off the ground. He carried the rock back to the Persian camp while the Persian soldiers crowded around him, cheering. Rostam took the rock to the space in front of Kavus's pavilion and there set it down.

"Here is your enemy, O my king. What shall we do with him?" said Rostam.

Kavus stared at the great rock, still in awe at Rostam's feat. "I'm not sure what we can do. We don't have any demonic magic to turn him back into a man."

"Right, then I'll deal with him." Rostam turned to the rock. "Get rid of this silly disguise and face your fate like a man. If you don't, I'll get axes and crowbars and turn you into a big pile of pebbles."

The rock dissolved first into mist and then reformed itself as a trembling man clad in armor.

Rostam seized his arm and dragged him in front of Kavus, saying, "Look! Here is that boulder, that mighty crag, who quivers into mist when he hears about my ax!"

Kavus looked long at the King of Mazandaran and said, "I see nothing in you that would merit a kingdom. You are but a coward who played at being king." Then Kavus turned to his soldiers. "Take him away and execute him."

So, the King of Mazandaran was duly taken out of the camp and beheaded.

Kavus sent some of his soldiers over to the Mazandaran camp to see that any money, jewels, armor, or weapons were collected and piled into heaps. He then had all his soldiers come to him one by one to receive their payment, and to those who had suffered the most, he gave the most. Any demons who refused to acknowledge Kavus as king were taken away and executed. When all this work was done, Kavus went away from the camp and spent a week praying to God and thanking him for his victory. On the eighth day, he summoned anyone who might have need and gave generously to them out of his treasury.

Before returning home, Kavus declared a week of rejoicing.

"Let there be feasts and music and dancing, and let the wine flow freely! God has given us the victory, so let us celebrate!" he said.

Rostam went to the king during one of the feasts and said, "O my king, I wish to speak to you of Olad."

"Yes, tell me of him," said Kavus.

"I captured Olad and made him my guide. He was faithful and never led me wrong. We owe part of our victory to him. I promised him that he could be king of this land if we defeated Mazandaran, and I would like to keep my word to him."

"Yes, you certainly should keep your word. Bring Olad and the Mazandaran elders and chieftains before me tomorrow, and we shall give your friend his reward."

Thus, on the next day, the elders and chieftains of Mazandaran swore fealty to Olad, and Olad was crowned King of Mazandaran, subject to the King of Persia.

When all this was done, Kavus returned home to his kingdom.

Kavus's Homecoming and Rostam's Reward

Kavus's army marched home, triumphant to the sound of drums and trumpets. When the people saw that Kavus had returned, they streamed out of the city, cheering and singing his praises. The whole country gave itself up to rejoicing. Every place was full of the sound of music, and feast followed feast for an entire week.

The first thing Kavus did when he retook his throne was open the treasury and give sums of money to every household in his kingdom. For this purpose, he appointed special messengers and treasurers to ensure that everyone got their share. For Rostam, there were special gifts: A crown and throne of his very own, beautiful maidservants, fiery horses, rich clothing and jewelry, and sacks of gold and pearls. However, the greatest reward of all was the throne of Sistan.

Kavus crowned Rostam himself, saying, "Only a kingdom of your own is a fit reward since you restored to me my kingdom."

When all the festivities were over, Rostam returned to Sistan, where he ruled wisely and well.

Kavus, for his part, dispensed justice and mercy upon his people to the end of his days.

Here's another book by Matt Clayton that you might like

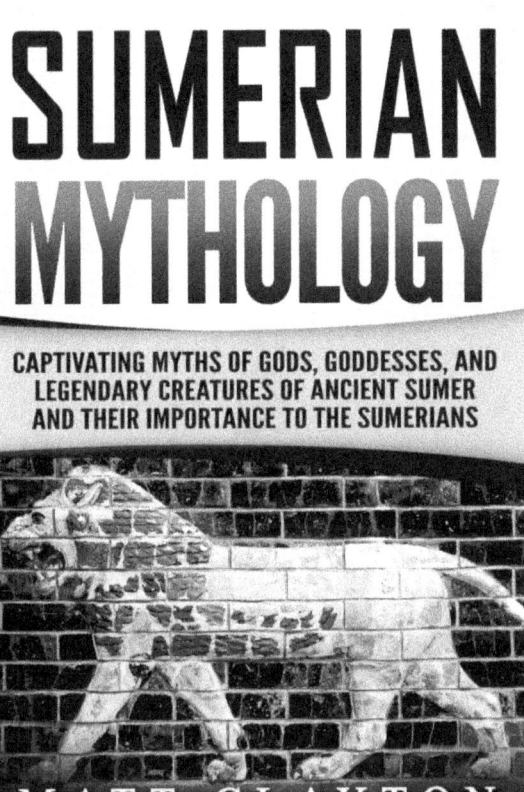

Free Bonus from Captivating History (Available for a Limited time)

Hi History Lovers!

Now you have a chance to join our exclusive history list so you can get your first history ebook for free as well as discounts and a potential to get more history books for free! Simply visit the link below to join.

Captivatinghistory.com/ebook

Also, make sure to follow us on Facebook, Twitter and Youtube by searching for Captivating History.

Bibliography

Anklesaria, Behramgore Temuras, trans. *Zand-Akasih: Iranian or Greater Bundahishn*. Bombay: n. p., 1956. Digital edition by Joseph H. Peterson, 2002. <http://www.avesta.org/mp/grb.htm> Accessed 16 December 2020.

Bleeck, Arthur Henry. *Avesta: The Religious Books of the Parsees*. 3 vols. Hertford: Stephen Austin, 1864.

Boyce, Mary, ed. and trans. *Textual Sources for the Study of Zoroastrianism*. Chicago: University of Chicago Press, 1984.

Citizen of Philadelphia, trans. *Bakhtiar Nameh, or The Royal Foundling: A Persian Story Exhibiting a Portraiture of Society in the East*. Philadelphia: Edward Parker, 1813.

Darmesteter, James, ed. and trans. *The Zend-Avesta*. 2nd ed. Oxford: Clarendon Press, 1895.

Eliade, Mircea. *Gods, Goddesses, and Myths of Creation: A Thematic Sourcebook of the History of Religion*. Part I: *From Primitives to Zen*. New York: Harper & Row, 1974.

Ferdowsi, Abolqasem. *Shahnameh: The Persian Book of Kings*. Dick Davis, trans. New York: Viking Penguin, 2006.

Keith, A. Barriedale, and Albert J. Carnoy. *Mythology of All Races*. Vol. 6: *Indian and Iranian*. Boston: Marshall Jones Company, 1917.

Ouseley, Sir William. *Bakhtyar Nameh, or Story of Prince Bakhtyar and the Ten Viziers*. London: Wilson & Co., 1801.

Rogers, Alexander, trans. *The Shah-namah of Fardusi*. 2 vols. London: Chapman & Hall, 1907.

Sykes, Ella C. *The Story-Book of the Shah, or Legends of Old Persia*. London: John MacQueen, 1901.

Warner, Arthur George, and Edmond Warner, trans. *The Shahnama of Firdausi*. 9 vols. London: K. Paul, Trench, Trübner & Co., Ltd., 1905.

West, Edward Wilson, trans. *Sacred Books of the East*. Vol. 5: *Pahlavi Texts*, Part I: *The Bundahis, Bahman Yast, and Shayast La-Shayast*. Oxford: Clarendon Press, 1880.

Wilson, Epiphanius. *Sacred Books of the East, Including Selections from the Vedic Hymns, the Zend-Avesta, the Dhammapada, the Upanishads, the Life of the Buddha, and the Koran*. London: The Colonial Press, 1902.

www.ingramcontent.com/pod-product-compliance
Lightning Source LLC
Chambersburg PA
CBHW050513240426
43673CB00004B/203